PRAISE FOR
THE POWER OF 100!

"Did you know that there's a blueprint for becoming a hero? In *The Power of 100!*, Shaun King helps everyday leaders discover the energy and ideas they need to realize their deepest passions and most important dreams. Crack open this book, strap on your cape, and soar."

> —Joshua DuBois, author, *The President's Devotional*, former executive director of the Office of Faith-based and Neighborhood Partnerships in the Executive Office of the President of the United States

"Passion is great, but eventually it has to lead to a plan or you'll only end up with a lot of what-might-have-been moments. Fortunately, Shaun King has created a personal, practical resource to help dreamers, achievers, and leaders accomplish the goals they've always felt called to!"

> —Jon Acuff, *New York Times* bestselling author of *Start: Punch Fear in the Face, Escape Average & Do Work That Matters*

"When it comes to making a difference in the world, Shaun King knows that it starts with leading yourself, with setting smart goals and going after them. I have learned so much from him and know you will, too. It all begins with understanding the power of 100."

—Jeff Goins, author, *The Art of Work*

"We're all guilty of backing away from a dream that seems impossible. I was almost moved to tears by the conviction I felt while reading Shaun's words about the fear and doubt we get once we 'grow up.' In this book Shaun not only makes you reenergize those ridiculous dreams you have, but he also gives practical steps on how to realistically achieve them. I'm going to keep this one close!"

—PJ Morton, Grammy winner, member of Maroon 5

"Success is nothing without a plan. If you are like me, a leader with many great ideas, you need help with how to see them manifested. *The Power of 100!* by Shaun King has amazing tools to get you right where you want to be."

—Ledisi, eight-time Grammy nominee

"Shaun King does the work and is who we say we should see more of. This book, with so many amazing stories and lessons from his life, is going to help you."

—Talib Kweli, hip-hop artist, activist

THE POWER OF
100!

KICKSTART YOUR DREAMS, BUILD MOMENTUM, AND DISCOVER UNLIMITED POSSIBILITY

SHAUN KING

HOWARD BOOKS
A DIVISION OF SIMON & SCHUSTER, INC.

NEW YORK   NASHVILLE   LONDON   TORONTO   SYDNEY   NEW DELHI

Howard Books
A Division of Simon & Schuster, Inc.
1230 Avenue of the Americas
New York, NY 10020

First Howard Books hardcover edition January 2015

HOWARD and colophon are trademarks of Simon & Schuster, Inc.

For information about special discounts for bulk purchases, please contact Simon & Schuster Special Sales at 1-866-506-1949 or business@simonandschuster.com.

The Simon & Schuster Speakers Bureau can bring authors to your live event. For more information or to book an event, contact the Simon & Schuster Speakers Bureau at 1-866-248-3049 or visit our website at www.simonspeakers.com.

Interior design by Jaime Putorti

Manufactured in the United States of America

10 9 8 7 6 5 4 3 2 1

Library of Congress Cataloging-in-Publication Data

King, Shaun, 1979–
 The power of 100! : kickstart your dreams, Build Momentum, and discover Unlimited possibility / Shaun King.
   pages cm
 ISBN 978-1-4767-9016-9
 1. Goal (Psychology) 2. Success–Psychological aspects. I. Title. II. Title: Keep it one hundred.
 BF505.G6K557 2015
 158–dc23   2014025823

ISBN 978-1-4767-9018-3
ISBN 978-1-4767-9017-6 (ebook)

To my beautiful best friend, Rai.

You've had my back since '97 and have encouraged me to pursue

my passions at every stop along the way.

Thank you, baby. I love you so much.

CONTENTS

PART C

THE SEVEN INTERLOCKING LIFE-GOAL CATEGORIES: LIFTING UP YOUR ENTIRE LIFE

PART D

HOW TO SEAL THE DEAL: MAKING YOUR 100 LIFE GOALS STICK

FOREWORD

For some reason we avoid thinking about death. It's as if we truly believe it will never occur to us. It's almost delusional.

But as I grow older, I gain more clarity on the human condition. I realize life is more than a series of chaotic events slammed together. It's more than time passing and experiences had. And it's more than fading away at an old age.

Over the past few years, it's been my mission alongside leaders like Shaun to help people escape the ordinary and to encourage them toward the life they love. At our core, humans desire purpose, connection, variety, and freedom. Yet many still find themselves locked in careers, cities, and bodies they dislike.

Why? Have we given up? Have we settled for typical? What shift in thinking have we allowed to creep into our hearts and minds?

Shaun's *The Power of 100!* unlocks the secrets for producing a wholesome life, a life of adventure and deep relationships and faith. Shaun offers simplicity, where many only bring complexity. His system is practical, functional, and proven. Even more, I've watched Shaun live out this book in his own life. From his exotic travels and fathering his large family to launching companies and building exciting relationships, his life is his research, and his dedication has continued to walk thousands down the path of purposeful living and authentic joy.

In the words to come, you'll learn that crafting a great life is not difficult; it's intentional. But we require a guide. A tool to assist us on our journey and to sustain our efforts. Here is your answer. It's more than a book. It's more than a plan. It's wisdom and opportunity bleeding from a page.

It's an answer to what really matters: your life.

To a story you want,

Dale Partridge, founder of TheDailyPositive.com
and Sevenly.org, author of *People Over Profit*

PREFACE

I smelled smoke. I tasted my blood and could feel the skin falling off my face. I strained to move my mouth and realized that it was full of glass. Jagged, large chunks of my teeth were missing. I thought I was going to die.

Just moments earlier everything on my checklist for a perfect life seemed to be in place:

New car? Check.

A good credit score? Yes.

Brand-new house? Check that one, too.

A fulfilling job that paid the bills? Check.

A church we loved? Definitely.

Some pocket money? Check.

A happy wife? Check.

A healthy baby? Yes indeed.

Seriously? What more could I ask for?

As I drove down the Kentucky interstate with my wife, Rai (pronounced "Ray"), that wintry Friday evening in November, my heart was full, my mind was clear, and I was one happy dude. We were visiting our family for Thanksgiving and had woken up ridiculously early the following morning to hunt down those insane Black Friday sales, wandering all over Lexington to buy items for our very first family home. We had racked up deals and were scheduled to move into our house back in Atlanta in four days. After dinner, we hopped in the car to drive a couple of miles down the road for a movie date with my brother and his wife.

It seemed like the perfect day.

Blasting from the speakers of the car was a fast-paced gospel song that we loved. I hardly ever listened to gospel music, but this song was our jam! Rai and I were both laughing and screaming the lyrics like crazy. The hook of the song says, "The presence of the Lord is here," and no one could tell me I didn't sound exactly like the dude on the record as I sang along with him. When the track ended, I did what any respectable man does when his favorite song ends . . . I reached down and hit the repeat button, so we could sing along just one more time.

In that instant the entire trajectory of my life changed. Within a second of restarting the song, the tires of our sedan hit an invisible patch of black ice. At sixty-five miles per hour the car began to spin out of control right through the middle of the interstate. I kid you not, with every fiber of my heart, soul, hands, and feet I tried to will that car straight, but I just couldn't do it.

Today, as I write these words, that stretch of road has a guardrail separating northbound and southbound traffic (maybe because of us), but back then it didn't. Nothing but a steep ditch divided the flow of cars in each direction. Our black Mitsubishi was careening straight for the divide, completely out of control. When we hit the ditch, the impact was so jarring that it alone likely gave us both concussions. Unfortunately, it wasn't enough to stop my car, and according to eyewitness accounts I read in the police report, we barreled out of the ditch and went airborne (*Dukes of Hazzard* style) into oncoming traffic.

Seeing the headlights of a large pickup truck coming full steam toward her door, my poor wife screamed out, "We're going to die!"

It was surreal.

Suddenly, it felt as if a bomb had gone off. I was confused. *How could a bomb have gone off in the car?* I wondered. It seemed like something had detonated directly before my eyes. Nothing else made any sense. It must have been a bomb!

In a matter of moments my perfect life exploded right in front of me.

Flesh was falling from my face.

I smelled smoke.

My mouth was full of blood and glass.

Jagged chunks of my teeth were missing.

I couldn't understand everything that was happening. But did I know things were really bad? Absolutely.

Still conscious, I glanced over at my wife and realized that I could hardly see. I tried to ask her if she was okay, but so much was terribly wrong with me. In my mind I wanted to talk to her, but my mouth just refused to form the words.

As the shock of the impact wore off, I realized my glasses were gone, and it felt like something unthinkable had happened to my left eye. I wondered if it was even still there. My wife, barely conscious and apparently in a state of shock, just stared at me. She didn't move or say a word.

That shook me.

Suddenly, I felt pain, *unthinkable* pain, covering my entire body and particularly all over my face. The desire to observe my surroundings faded away.

The excruciating pain took over.

Of course a bomb had not gone off in our car that night. Instead, we had collided with a large pickup truck. At the last moment, by no ingenuity of my own, I had been able to swerve just enough to keep the truck from killing my wife as she sat helplessly in the front seat next to me. However, the sheer force of the collision crushed our little car.

I was ejected through the windshield, not headfirst but face-first into the dense glass. To this day, I can't even believe that's possible. The instant my face crashed through the thick windshield, we hit a guardrail on the opposite side of the interstate. The blunt impact and miraculously perfect timing flung my body back into the car.

The car was now a mangled mess on the side of the road, my face felt like it was on fire, and I began to roar loud moans of pain. With each wail, I felt weaker and weaker. My whole body was wet. It was my blood.

A man came to my door. *Yes! He's going to save me*, I thought. Instead, he simply looked at me and left. My heart sank. The roads were pretty empty that night, and I wondered if anyone else would come and help us. Oddly enough, there was no trace of that man in any of the reports from that evening. One of my "ultra-religious" friends insists that he was an angel of death who came to take me away. Whoever it was, he left me alone there and never returned.

About a minute later, the sweetest woman came to my car. I know for sure that she was human, but I swear she felt like an angel! She couldn't open the door, but she told me that she was a nurse at the University of Kentucky hospital and that she wasn't going to leave my side until an ambulance arrived. She said I was very badly injured and that she needed to wrap my mangled face up with a blanket she'd seen in the backseat to hopefully slow my bleeding. My leg felt like it had been crushed somehow, and everything from my shoulders up still seemed like it was on fire.

A police officer arrived and asked me my name and whom to contact in my family. I was able to mumble my name and give him my dear mother's phone number. Then they cut me out of the car, carefully lifted me onto a stretcher, and put me in the ambulance. I missed my wife immediately. I began to believe that I might never see her again.

What happened in the back of that ambulance for the next fifteen minutes is the reason I've written this book and also why I want to help you squeeze value out of every precious moment of every day you have left on earth.

On TV, the paramedics are always so doggone calm and cool. Maybe paramedics are normally that way in real life, too, but the two guys in the back of that ambulance with me were nervous wrecks! I heard them talking about the broken bones in my face. One of the guys said my left leg appeared broken. They wondered aloud if I had a traumatic brain injury. I heard them nervously conferring about my heart rate slowing, and it seemed like I was slipping away.

Was I dying? I saw no white light. My heart was overcome with a heavy sadness. The pain disappeared.

I was only twenty-three years old.

I would never get to see my daughter, Kendi, grow up. She'd never know me. I loved her so much.

Rai had always told me that she wanted to travel the world, and I had hardly even taken her anywhere yet.

We had no money in our savings account.

I felt like a failure. I didn't even get to tell them good-bye. I was sure that God had plans for my life that required me to live so far beyond that painful night. I was bewildered. Everything became darker, and I found it harder and harder to sustain a coherent thought.

"Stick with us, man!" I heard one of the paramedics yell. I was trying. "We're going to get you to the hospital, and they'll take care of you. Just stick with us, bro."

The two men in the back with me then started arguing with the driver to hurry up. "You're going too damn slow. You have to hurry up, man," one of them said to the driver. The driver yelled back, "Shut up! The roads are icy as hell. I can't drive fast, or we'll all be like him."

I found myself just wanting to go to sleep. I was so tired.

At my drowsiest moment, I heard the guys ask each other if they should "charge the paddles," and I remember being scared to death that they were going to use them on me. To this day, I think my overwhelming fear of the paramedics' placing those electrically charged paddles on my chest gave me all the motivation I needed to stay conscious.

From that moment forward, I don't recall anything else the guys said to me or to each other. All I remember is a thought in my head that I kept playing over and over and over again: *If I make it to the hospital, I'll live. If I make it there, everything will be okay.*

At that point, my mind turned not to what *I* could do, but to the hope and prayer that God would just get us safely to the doctors so that I could live.

I did not want to die.

I don't think I made a grand bargain with God that night, but I remember thinking, *If I don't die, if I make it, if I live, I'm going to give life everything I have from here on out.*

As soon as we made it to the University of Kentucky ER, I was overtaken with a feeling of warmth. It's hard to explain, but I felt a deep sense of inner peace, contentment, and even joy. I could no longer see out of either of my eyes or really feel my face at all. I felt them cutting my clothes off with scissors. Hilariously, I still remember being slightly embarrassed that people were going to see me naked. After examining my body, I heard the ER doctors speaking about the bones in my face being broken and how I would need a plastic surgeon. They ordered immediate CAT scans to determine the extent of the damage.

The damage to my lips, mouth, and teeth was so severe that I wouldn't be able to speak for much longer once they started working on me. I began begging two different nurses to write a note that said, "I still believe in the goodness of God," and place it on my chest. They both thought I was delirious and refused to write it. I asked several more times, but I am sure I sounded ridiculous.

Finally, I felt and grabbed the hand of a third person and asked them to please write the note. They relented, grabbed a piece of paper, wrote the words just as I asked, and placed it right on my chest.

For the next three days I could hardly think straight, but I remember asking everybody who came into contact with me to read that note.

As the doctors sent me through the first set of CAT scans, the results shocked everyone, because *nothing* was broken. Seeing how badly shredded every inch of my face was, the doctors ordered another set of scans. They, too, came back with the same results. In spite of flying into the windshield face-first, going full speed, and being hit by a truck, not one bone in my body, not even my nose, was broken.

Then and there, the doctors started calling me a "miracle man."

Kneeling down to talk to me on the stretcher, the plastic surgeon said, "I had already asked my team to get plates and wires ready for your face, but it appears that we were all wrong and that you aren't going to need them after all. Rarely do people in accidents like yours—being projected through the windshield—rarely do those people live. When they do live, they are almost always paralyzed and need a series of reconstructive surgeries to attempt to repair the damage. It appears that all I have to do is stitch you up."

I pointed at the note on my chest. I couldn't muster a smile, but I knew then and there that something miraculous had indeed happened to me. I can't explain it.

Was I healed?

Was everybody wrong with their diagnoses?

How did my face crash completely through that rock-hard windshield without breaking a single bone?

Why me?

For the next two hours, the plastic surgeon worked magic on my face. He started out by giving me a few extremely excruciating shots of Novocain to dull the pain of the procedure. When it was all said and done, he ended up giving me over forty shots. Bit by bit, he pulled over one hundred small shards of glass out of my face. During the next four weeks I removed over a dozen more.

My left eyelid had been cut off almost completely, and he sewed it back on first. A huge chunk of my bottom lip was dangling. He fixed that next. On the left side of my face was the most severe injury. My cheek had been torn open from the corner of my mouth all the way up to my left ear. In all, my face required over four hundred stitches to be put back together again. My eyes would be swollen shut for days. I couldn't eat. My teeth were all jacked up. People who see pictures of me taken several days later say I looked like a dead man. Physically, I felt dead, but something deep inside of me was awakened. In so many ways, I now view my life in two phases: BTA (Before the Accident) and ATA (After the Accident).

I valued life before all this happened. I was a good enough guy and did some decent stuff here and there, but something essential changed about me after the car crash. It's this transformation that allows me to look back on that brutal brush with death and not regret that I went through it. Yes, it took a lot out of me. Physically, I never fully recovered. I'm actually in pain as I type these very words. However, what I gained was so much greater than what was taken from me.

Now I live like tomorrow's not promised.

Now I live like every day is a blessing full of 1,440 minutes to pursue my purpose and passion.

Now I refuse to allow the excuses in my mind to grow into giants that keep me from living up to my full potential.

Having come so close to death, I now value just how precious life truly is and want to ride what God gave me until the wheels fall off. The American dream alone is not enough for me anymore.

Just a few weeks after the accident, with my body still hurting and my face looking so awful that people everywhere stopped to stare at me, I found my heart, soul, and mind energized anew. I've hardly stopped for a break since.

At first, I had no method to my madness. I found myself energized, but with no real system to effectively pursue what it was on my heart to accomplish in the world.

I've had some unbelievable successes, and I've also learned painful lessons through failures so low I can hardly stand to think of them. This book is about those hard-earned lessons I learned, the practical systems that I'm using now, and how they can help you rapidly accelerate the impact you make with the time you have. My hope is that together we will start a movement of thousands (maybe millions!) of people setting and pursuing their life goals with reckless abandon.

INTRODUCTION

WHY 100?

I'm from the hip-hop generation.

Hip-hop was born when I was born, and it has grown and matured as I've grown and matured. When I was a kid in the eighties, listening to the Fat Boys and the Rappin' Duke, it was hard to imagine seeing or hearing hip-hop in every other commercial, rappers onstage at the stuffy Tony Awards, or Dr. Dre becoming a billionaire by selling his company to Apple. It has now become so mainstream that we could argue hip-hop is America's biggest cultural contribution to the world since Hollywood or jazz.

No number is more quintessentially hip-hop than 100. This has been fueled, no doubt, by the frequent lyrical mentioning of one-hundred-dollar bills, but the number 100 has taken on a powerful meaning and life of its own in a way that I hope inspires you. Today, when a rapper says to "keep it 100," it means to be the highest, best expression of yourself. "Keeping it 100" is even a step above the hip-hop phrase "keeping it real," which is all about being honest. When Jay Z says he's "keeping it 100" in the songs

"DOA" and "Part II (On the Run)," it's his way of telling you not only that he's being truthful, but that what he is saying is a form of power-truth, with no wiggle room or ambiguity, in a culture that permits exaggeration more than ever. In fact, because rap—and life outside of rap, for that matter—is so full of fakery, when a rapper tells you he is "keeping it 100," it's his way of separating fact from fiction.

The title of this book, *The Power of 100!*, is, without a doubt, inspired by my love for and relationship with hip-hop, but more than just a colloquial phrase, it honestly describes my greatest wish for you as the reader. The life you are leading is likely more of a diminished version of your best self than you understand. Most of us are fully aware that we are not "keeping it 100" with our dreams, aspirations, and goals. Most of us are fully aware that we aren't "keeping it 100" with our finances and our fitness. You know and I know that you aren't "keeping it 100" with the ideas and impressions that are on your heart to pursue. We live far beneath our human potential and too often settle for a shell, a carbon copy, a knockoff counterfeit version of who we could truly become if we put everything we had into crafting and pursuing our life goals. When I tell you to "keep it 100," it's not because I think you are a liar but because I believe a truer, better version of your life is out there waiting to be lived.

In American culture, the grade of 100 represents excellence and maximum effort. If a restaurant receives a score of 100 from the health inspectors, it's a boost for the business. 100 means your device is at full power. If a movie receives the rare score of 100 on Rotten Tomatoes, it is filmmaking perfection. If a child receives a grade of 100 on a science test, parents are elated. Wilt Chamberlain's scoring 100 points in a single basketball game is held up as the highest level of performance in the sport.

So how can we achieve our own 100? I am inviting you on a journey, a journey on which we will be working together to carefully craft 100 life goals, to catch vision and pursue it with reckless abandon. Long before I created 100 life goals of my own, John Goddard, the father of life goals, wrote his down in 1940 and spent the rest of his life pursuing them until he passed away in 2013. Inspired by John Goddard and also by Ted Leonsis, the current owner of the Washington Wizards and Washington Capitals (basketball and hockey) sports franchises, my friend Mark Batterson, pastor of National Community Church in Washington, DC, wrote down 100 life goals of his own and started blogging about how it changed his life. Encouraged by these three men, I started setting and pursuing 100 life goals of my own. The following year, completely hooked on the idea, I developed a curriculum to begin helping others create 100 life goals and have since taught tens of thousands of people about the importance of living with intention.

So, while I can't promise you that if you "keep it 100" you will become even a slightly better rapper, I can absolutely assure you that you'll have a lot more to rap about. The system I'm sharing here will help you set and pursue 100 life goals across seven key areas of your life. More than a bucket list, this is a well-formulated strategy on how to go after your hopes and dreams for the rest of your days. It will change your life completely, if you'll let it.

In the truest sense, what follows is a "workbook." Yes, I need you to read it, but I also need you to work it.

I'm going to ask you to take actual steps and make real life decisions.

I'm going to ask you to change your daily schedule.

I'm going to demand you stop some bad habits.

I'm asking you to trust that I won't guide you in the wrong direction. But I'm also here to help you beyond this book, and all of my contact information is in the back.

Now, let's get to work.

PART A

NO MORE EXCUSES

Time to Push the Reset Button

Ninety-nine percent of the failures come from people

who have the habit of making excuses.

—GEORGE WASHINGTON CARVER

He that is good for making excuses is seldom good for anything else.

—BENJAMIN FRANKLIN

Although no one can go back and make a brand-new start,

anyone can start from now and make a brand-new ending.

—CARL BARD

Ever had to completely reset your phone?

I don't mean rebooting it by turning the power off and back on; I'm talking about a hard, erase-everything-on-that-bad-boy type of reset. Normally this is the last resort. You've tried everything else you know to do. Nothing's working. The moment . . . that dreaded moment . . . it has arrived.

The only way to get your gadget back up and working again is to reset the whole doggone thing back to the factory settings. Of course you didn't back it up like you were supposed to. Who does? You're going to lose some important phone numbers and a few photos you wish you'd saved somewhere else, but it's time. You have to make a move. This slow thing is jamming you up.

Did you download a bad app? Are the settings screwed up? Do you just have too much junk in there? Whatever the problem, by pushing that reset button, we can pretty much guarantee that

what's ailing your device is going to go away. Pushing the reset button won't remove that scratch from the screen—it won't add even
an ounce of shine to the chrome—but you can live with that as long
as you can get it humming and working the way it was intended.

Maybe I'm just a weird tech nerd, but I even get a little excited
when I push that reset button. It's like the forbidden fruit of the
electronic world. Every other button gets pushed daily, but not this
one. It's hidden and special.

See that space above this sentence? I actually deleted three very
socially awkward lines about just how excited pushing the reset
button gets me. I reread them a few times and scared myself a
little!

What were we talking about again? Oh yeah! The reset button . . . *your* reset button. We aren't really talking about phones
here. This is about maximizing your life and your impact in the
world.

You and I both know that it's time to start some things over. I'm
not here to tell you that you suck or that your life is terrible. I'm
here to tell you that you were created and designed to be faster and
more productive than you are right now.

Somewhere along the way you downloaded some junk—some
bad apps, some spam, maybe even a virus or two. You are living so
far beneath your potential that it's time to quit making excuses and
start living your life on purpose!

It's time to hit the reset button.

I've had to reset my entire life on three different occasions. I can tell you it's never easy, but sometimes a fresh start is what it takes to get you back on track.

The next four chapters are going to kick your butt; just know that I'm doing it out of love. Excuses are the enemy of progress. If you are truly going to create and pursue a multitude of life goals with reckless abandon, your excuses must die. Together we're going to blow them to little bits and use what's left of your life to build the foundation for the new you!

I'm pumped up just thinking about it.

Get ready to push reset.

Are you ready? Let's roll!

A goal without a plan is just a wish.

—ANTOINE DE SAINT-EXUPÉRY

Where there is no vision, the people perish.

—PROVERBS 29:18 (KJV)

Give me six hours to chop down a tree,
and I will spend the first four sharpening the axe.

—ABRAHAM LINCOLN

You can always amend a big plan, but you can
never expand a little one. I don't believe in little plans.
I believe in plans big enough to meet a situation
which we can't possibly foresee now.

—HARRY TRUMAN

1

IF YOU HAD A PLAN

Preparing to Live Life on Purpose from Here on Out

Unless you spent an extended amount of time with me personally, it's unlikely that you'd ever discover how much physical pain I live with every single day.

I don't tweet about it much.

I try very hard to never allow it to slow me down or get in the way of living an adventurous life.

I don't show it to strangers or coworkers if I can help it, but I'm always hurting.

When I was fifteen, I was the victim of a brutal assault that caused me to miss nearly two years of high school recovering from three spinal surgeries and fractures to my face and ribs. I've had more surgeries since then to deal with the injuries and pain. The car crash didn't make it better. I've grown to accept that my pain is like that friend we all need who tells us the cold, hard truth about ourselves.

Sometimes my pain is so debilitating that I can hardly walk or get out of bed. It normally subsides after some extended rest, but one time a few years ago it just didn't go away.

A day turned into a week.

A week turned into a month.

I was worried in the worst way.

I was the primary breadwinner for my family. I had tried to get disability insurance several times, but providers wouldn't touch me because of my injuries. The doctors were suggesting that I have a multilevel spinal fusion, which could require a full year of recovery. The pain was so severe that two different doctors suggested I go ahead and have a drug pump permanently installed on my back to help me cope. Mortified at these options, I decided to get radical.

I hired a personal trainer—a man named Andrew Johnston who had kicked cancer's ass—and I started training to climb a mountain. At first glance, my wacky idea probably seemed to make no sense whatsoever. But every study I read explained that half of the people who had the surgery my doctors were recommending still lived in severe pain afterward anyway. Physical therapy hadn't really worked for me in the past, but I knew setting an audacious and halfway-frightening physical goal would be just the motivation I'd need to give overcoming my pain a real shot. I decided that if I was going to have surgery or wear a drug pump, it was going to be *after* I pushed myself to the limit and someone had to carry me to the ER on a stretcher. A few people thought my plan was the dumbest thing ever, but I knew that it was what I needed to get me going.

Sometimes you have to plan something audacious to change things. Nobody else is going to craft a plan for your life with as

much care and precision and boldness as you can. Surgeons plan
for surgery! They don't necessarily advise their patients to go to
mountaineering school, but I knew that if I didn't work a plan for
myself, somebody else was going to make plans for me that might
take me down a dangerous path far away from my dreams and passions.

I like to say it this way: not having plans really just means you
have plans that suck! If you don't plan out your life, someone else
will, and you will *never* be the centerpiece of anybody else's plans.

Are you hearing what I'm saying?

I can tell you right now with 100 percent certainty that you will
only achieve two or three life goals by accident until the day you
die. Life just doesn't work like that.

Nobody frees slaves by accident.

Nobody climbs Mount Everest by accident.

Nobody gets six-pack abs by accident.

Nobody starts a successful business by accident.

Nobody has an accidentally blissful marriage.

If you are going to go from where you are right now to the
extremely successful, high-performing version of yourself that I
want you to see in your mind, it's going to take a well-crafted strategic plan, a set of actionable instructions:
it's going to take a road map.

Hide your toes for a second. I'm
about to step on them. Just know that I
say what I say . . . because I've lived it.

You will only achieve two or three life goals by accident until the day you die.

Consciously or subconsciously, not having a hard-core life plan
gives you the emotional space and permission to never really suc-

ceed at home, on the job, with your health, with finances, or any-where else. If you don't really have a plan and basically choose to live out the plans of your boss or of societal norms, you give your-self a false sense of never really failing, because you didn't have a plan to work from in the first place. Yes, it's technically true that you can't lose a game that you don't play, but you sure as heck won't win it either.

Most people in the world are winging it right now—with no cred-ible life plan or road map or sense of direction to guide them. The dean of science fiction writers, Robert A. Heinlein, said it like this: "In the absence of clearly defined goals, we become strangely loyal to performing daily trivia until ultimately we become enslaved by it."

If you are reading this right now, I can only assume that you no longer want to be enslaved by the mundane daily trivia the world keeps throwing your way. You are tired of the rat race. You are fully and completely aware that you are better than your past, but you are smart enough to know that if you don't change how you do things you will keep getting the same old results year after year. Trust me, I want this for you, but I can't want you to change enough for it to actually happen. You are going to have to will your-self into a new way of doing life.

The first step to get in the game is to accept that you are going to have to take the time and energy to craft the most robust and effec-tive strategic life plan you've ever seen. There is no way around it.

Would you want an architect to build your dream home with no blueprints?

Would you want a teacher to spend eight hours a day with your children without well-prepared lessons?

Would you want a financial planner who manages your savings and investments to just wing it?

Would you want to eat a cake your kids baked without a recipe?

Would you want a government with no earthly idea how to navigate partisan bickering? (That's a joke!) Of course not!

You and I expect professionals to be trained and to have detailed, step-by-step plans on how to do what we are paying them to do, but we often put more energy and effort into planning what we are going to wear than how we are actually going to live. Our grocery lists are planned better than most of our lives!

Mediocrity is counting on you to keep this bad habit. Failure is pleading with you to live life without a strategy. Bad credit and poverty thrive on poor planning and pray you won't change.

This is about to get deep. . . .

The muscles of your body, mind, heart, and soul are so used to your not having a credible strategy for life that they are actually going to work against you in the form of self-sabotage in the weeks ahead. The plan we are about to create and that you are about to live is going to be such a radical departure from how you've always done things that everything in you is going to want to give up.

You think I'm lying, don't you?

You are going to start hearing voices telling you that this is a waste of time and that the way you've always done things has gotten you this far, so why change now?

In fact, I demand that you make a decision, right here and now, to reject the "normal" way of living life: flying by the seat of your pants, putting the cart before the horse. You are better than that, and the goals of your heart deserve better than that.

A few of you are even going to attempt to make a religious justification for not putting a life plan in place. Ever heard the phrase "God laughs at our plans"? That's not actually in the Bible! Back when I was a pastor, I knew a preacher who got up one Sunday morning and proceeded to quote a lyric from the beautiful song you may remember Luther Vandross singing, "A House Is Not a Home." There's nothing wrong with quoting a good song every now and then, but this guy said, "Like it says in the Bible, 'A house is not a home . . .'" Everybody started snickering, because the dude quoted an R & B star and attributed it to God!

The Bible, and most sacred texts for that matter, is full of examples of women and men who executed amazing plans. I'm not here to say that your plans won't shift and morph and grow organically over time, but don't blame God or angels or religion for your lack of planning.

I'd like for you to take a second right now to think of four people, past or present, whom you truly admire. They can be family members or international leaders we've all heard of before—they just need to mean something to you personally.

Here's my list:

- Civil rights leader Dr. Martin Luther King Jr.

- My mother, Kay King (no relation to Dr. King)

- Nineteenth-century abolitionist Harriet Tubman

- The founder of Twitter and Square, Jack Dorsey

Who are your four people? (Don't skip past this! Think of four people you admire right now!)

I could come up with twenty more off the top of my head, but I want you to get just a few in your mind for now. Have you noticed that those we tend to admire most are women and men who lived out the plans of their hearts?

The March on Washington and the Montgomery Bus Boycott were not accidents but strategically planned parts of a broad civil rights movement. Yes, Dr. King was an enormously gifted speaker, but lots of people have gifts. We know who Dr. King is because he worked his plan—even when it hurt, even when it was inconvenient, even when I am sure he had severe doubts about his safety and wondered if any of his plans were really worth pursuing. But Dr. King worked his plan to such perfection that *Time* magazine, forty-five years after his death, published a cover story declaring that he should be thought of as a "Founding Father" of the United States of America. Where would we be today if Dr. King had chosen comfort over courage? I don't even want to know.

My dear mother, who recently retired after forty-plus years of making lightbulbs at the Sylvania lamp plant in Versailles, Kentucky, had a plan for raising two sons who knew the value of hard work, so she didn't just tell us about it but lived it right in front of us, day in and day out. I remember seeing her come home drenched in sweat after each brutally hard day of making lightbulbs. It was far from glorious and most often harsh, but she had dreams and plans and they required her to push through her frustrations. (Now, Mom, I want to help you craft goals that don't involve Jason and me, okay?)

Can you imagine the level of audacious planning that went into the hidden network of homes and hiding places we know as the Underground Railroad during the days of American slavery? Harriet Tubman, risking her own capture, ventured back into slaveholding states, often in the dark of night, to help free men, women, and children from forced bondage. Simply being a free black woman in the age of slavery was hard enough all by itself, but Harriet Tubman had plans that were bigger than her comfort.

Jack Dorsey could have simply been satisfied with the fact that he helped take Twitter from a seed of an idea to a platform used all over the planet, but he didn't stop at that. With nothing more than a napkin sketch of an iPhone with something resembling an acorn stuck in the headphone jack, Jack Dorsey took his basic idea of a mobile payment solution powered by a smartphone and made plans for how to actually execute the brilliantly simple idea he called Square—now one of the top payment-processing companies in the world, used by businesses everywhere.

The fact of the matter is that Dr. King, my dear mother, Harriet Tubman, and Jack Dorsey all faced outrageous odds before they ever got started. They aren't amazing because they lived lives without obstacles or mistakes. They are amazing because they had hopes and dreams and plans that they valued much more than any hurdle thrown their way. I know enough about each of them to say that very few people would have criticized them if they had refused to take some of the huge risks that were required of them to fight for their beliefs.

Had Harriet Tubman freed just one person from bondage, it would have been amazing, but that was not her plan! Had Dr. King stopped the Montgomery Bus Boycott after 100 or 200 days, people would have understood this decision, but he and others painfully carried it on for 381 days! They were jailed, beaten, humiliated, and even fired from their jobs until the laws changed, giving everyone equal access to public transportation. At your lowest moment in life, having a plan in place will give you the hope, the light at the end of the tunnel, the anchor, the foundation to push through the doubt and despair you will surely face.

Maybe you feel like good opportunities never come your way. Maybe you feel like you have bad luck.

Maybe you feel like you are too old or too broke or too afraid to even set out on the journey we are about to begin.

I'm calling you out on all of that.

Malcolm Gladwell, in his book *David and Goliath: Underdogs, Misfits, and the Art of Battling Giants*, declares that society has greatly overestimated the value of a silver spoon and that being thought of as a superpower in the world (while it may have a few benefits) has many disadvantages that can open opportunities for regular people who learn to see being small and nimble as an asset rather than a liability.

So no more excuses.

More than anything else, when you finish reading and working *The Power of 100!* you are going to come out on the other side of the journey with the best life plan you've ever developed.

In 2006, I started to sense that I had hit a glass ceiling at my job. The entire work environment there was incredibly toxic. The best employees were grossly underpaid and underappreciated. Unfortunately, many of them had put themselves in the precarious position of not having skills that applied to the real world outside of this company, and consequently, I saw employees (many of whom had worked there for ten to fifteen years) stay on board in spite of their personal and professional misery because they just didn't know what else to do.

I wasn't going to let that happen to me.

I knew that I had to have skills and a network that stretched beyond my current place of employment. I started a blog and decided to throw all of my extra energy into social media. Twitter had just launched, and back then it was a place for about a million or so geeks and nerds to gather. Almost eight years later, I had started two social media companies, sold them both, and raised millions of dollars for good causes all over the world through Twitter, Facebook, and YouTube. Social media has almost exclusively paid my bills for the past three years. What began as a hunch when I felt my back was against the wall became my hobby and eventually my career!

But before I ever made a living in the world of social media, I had a plan.

Many more excuses are bound to creep in over the next few crucial days and weeks as we reset and begin the new you. I want you to draw a line in the sand now, committing to the belief that while money, fear, and time may be legitimate issues as we begin, flopping at life because of the lack of an actionable plan is no longer acceptable for you.

We're killing that excuse here and now.

It's dead.

Together, we are going to craft a bulletproof life plan that leapfrogs past every issue and excuse that has held you back all these years.

The truth is, with a plan:

You could have a PhD in ten years.

You could be a doctor in seven years.

You could be a lawyer in three.

You could be a millionaire and purchase your home with cash.

You could be so fit that you run the Ironman triathlon in two years.

You could be physically rescuing men and women from modern-day slavery next year.

By the end of this year, you could double the quality of life for your family and take vacations they'll never forget.

You could open up a profitable business in six months.

I'm going to say this a lot, but I can pretty much guarantee that none of the things I just named are going to happen by accident. If you work today to carefully craft and pursue your 100 life goals, the entire trajectory of your life will change in powerful ways.

You are going to put yourself on a path of awareness and preparation unlike anything you've experienced. It's going to make you more ready than you've ever been to actually achieve your goals. That awareness and preparation that you gain is going to open up a floodgate of opportunities for you.

I've heard Oprah (and many other people) say it like this: "Luck is preparation meeting opportunity." We are actually blind to opportunities when we are not fully prepared to seize them. It's not that new opportunities are going to be created for you all the time (although this will happen more than ever), but you are finally going to have the right mind-set to recognize them.

When you are prepared to see opportunities, your "luck" changes drastically. You become a factory of good luck, and people start to wonder why good things *always* happen to you. It's all in how you see things, how you mix the right ingredients for luck and success.

Imagine, for a moment, that you are going to live to be eighty-five years old. At the age I am writing this I would have fifty years of life yet to live. In that time, I could write fifty more books. I could travel to every country in the world. I could learn to fly a plane. I could become a world-class chef. In essence, if I chose to take a long view of my life and put a hard-core plan in place, I could do anything in the world I wanted to do. The flip side of this is also true. How insanely sad would it be to live to be eighty-five years old and not accomplish any of your life goals, having dibble-dabbled your life away? I refuse to let that be my story, and I don't want it to be yours either. Let's make the transition from letting the whims of the world lead us, day in and day out, to living a deliberate, purpose-filled life.

Before we get started, though, we need to straighten out two critical ideas.

First, a plan is *not* a list.

Lists aren't terrible and I guess they are better than nothing, but you can't guide your life from a list. When we are done crafting your life goals, we will have a real strategy for how and when you'll pursue each of them and how achieving certain goals will unlock the skills and resources and network to achieve many more of the goals you've crafted. Each of your life goals may have lists of action items and notes under it, but a list in and of itself is not a plan.

Here's what I mean. You might say, "I'm hungry."

Being hungry is not a plan—it's a feeling.

So maybe your next thought is, *I need to go to the grocery store.*

While that idea has a little more clarity than "I'm hungry," it's still not a plan.

Here's a plan: "This morning from 8 a.m. to 9 a.m. I am going to make a grocery list of what we need. Then I'm going to go grocery shopping this afternoon and spend $300 on groceries from that list at Costco and Whole Foods. I'll eat lunch at Whole Foods before I shop and have a budget of $15 for my lunch."

Much more specific than a general idea, a plan gets you where you need to go and takes care of you once you get there.

Second, goals can be fueled by dreams, but they aren't the same thing. A goal is a dream with a timeline and action steps.

When we craft your plan of action and your 100 life goals, we're not just going to jot down thoughts or pie-in-the-sky ideas. We may start off that way, but each goal is going to require a foundation of ingredients and action items that give it a real sense of direction. For instance, when we dig into your financial goals, "I need to make more money" will not be an acceptable goal. If you made $5 a week **A goal is a dream with a timeline and action steps.** more, that would technically mean you made more money, but that's not strong enough to be a life goal. A great starting point for a financial goal would be, "I will completely pay off my credit card debt in twenty-four months" or "I will increase my income by $15,000 a year in less than thirty-six months." With those goals, we have a starting point, a timeline, and a destination. They are measurable, and with those points of information, we will be able to really dig in together to determine what has to happen to make those goals a reality.

At the end of the day, I need you to begin making the mental shift to living life on purpose, with a plan and a true, well-thought-out sense of direction. Built into your plan will be plenty of space for spontaneity, course corrections, and the inevitable fact that you will change your mind regularly! However, I need you to be clear on this—your full, unwavering acceptance of the necessity of a strong action plan is the foundation of the work that lies ahead. The plan that we are going to create together will get you through painful seasons of doubt. When your money is funny, your schedule is overbooked, and you feel like throwing in the towel, this plan will be an essential tool to keep your heart and mind from giving up.

It's a little like how my first mountaineering experience went. It was brutal. It kicked my butt, but I loved it. I learned more in those five days about mountaineering and about myself than I ever expected. I gave everything I had to that mountain, and in the end my plan to avoid spinal fusion worked! Not only did I learn the essential skills I needed to climb virtually any mountain in the world, the fitness and core strength I gained from my time on Mount Baker has allowed me to be surgery-free now for nearly fifteen years.

I still have good days and bad days like the next person, but I'm living out my dreams and achieving more and more of my own life goals right now because I have a plan in place. As I reflect back over the past fifteen years, I can tell you that when I was flying by the seat of my pants, I often found myself broke and disappointed. When I had a strategic plan and a real sense of direction, I went farther and higher than I ever imagined.

Do one thing every day that scares you.

—ELEANOR ROOSEVELT

There is only one thing that makes a dream impossible to achieve: the fear of failure.

—PAULO COELHO

Logic will get you from A to Z; imagination will get you everywhere.

—ALBERT EINSTEIN

Man often becomes what he believes himself to be. If I keep on saying to myself that I cannot do a certain thing, it is possible that I may end by really becoming incapable of doing it. On the contrary, if I have the belief that I can do it, I shall surely acquire the capacity to do it even if I may not have it at the beginning.

—MAHATMA GANDHI

2

IF YOU HAD NO FEAR

Regaining Your Imagination and Living Life with Gusto

Once you were a kid who would sing in front of people on demand—not because you had the chops of John Legend, but because you didn't care what people thought about you. You used to be willing to bust a move or dance a jig in front of everybody. You used to be willing to get your face painted like a zoo animal or a superhero and wear it all day long—just because it looked cool to you. You used to imagine yourself as president of the United States. You used to dream you'd be an astronaut. You used to believe you'd write songs and books and scripts that the whole world would love. You used to design clothes in your mind that set trends. You used to believe that you could be . . . whatever your heart was big enough to believe. Do you remember when your imagination was limitless?

Just yesterday, my only son, Ezekiel (we call him EZ), who's eight years old, asked me if he could play baseball for the Los

Angeles Dodgers (he's played half a season of Little League), play basketball for the Miami Heat (he's never played an organized game), be a stand-up comedian like Jim Gaffigan, and be a pastor. Of course I smiled and gave him a big emphatic *"Yes!"*—followed by a quick note about how hard he was going to have to work to do all these awesome things. He still sees his future as limitless, and I see it as beautiful. When Jesus told his disciples to have faith like children, I'm pretty sure he didn't mean to forget to flush the toilet and leave toys all over the place, but that we should have an unlimited imagination about what is possible in the world. However, being an adult seems to be all about tucking away your imagination and living a life full of limits. Don't you agree? Fear has pretty much squeezed all the imagination (and fun) out of us!

Consciously and subconsciously, fear is the primary reason we don't set goals and pursue them like our lives depend on it. Fear talks you out of your dreams. Fear talks you out of making radical life shifts like moving around the world or quitting your dead-end job. Fear causes you to believe that you don't have what it takes to turn your ideas into inventions. Fear convinces you that the businesses and charities you've dreamed up will never succeed or change the world. Fear talks you into a mundane daily routine of work and television with a little Internet thrown in there to spice things up.

As much as I'd love for you and me to dig right in to crafting an insane life plan, all of my experience with helping others pursue their dreams tells me that we will be wasting our time if we don't first tackle your fears head-on. If you are thinking right now that you don't have any fears, I personally diagnose you with the fear of telling the truth about yourself! All of us have fears. I have fears. My heroes had fears. We just don't let our fears outweigh our determination or push us into predictable mediocrity. You and I can craft the best life goals of all time, but without kicking fear in the face, they'll just become old dusty blueprints. In the following chapters we'll deal with the limitations of time and money, but even if you have unlimited time and cash, fear has the power to render those things useless. It must be addressed first.

Seven primary fears serve as psychological shackles for people all over the world. They have a stronghold on your mind and prevent you from tapping into your boundless potential. Some of these fears are going to really hit home for you, but the truth is that even the most successful and fulfilled people in the world are daily overcoming these fears or have already tackled them in the past. When your fears go unchecked, they become full-fledged phobias, and it's likely that one is holding you back in life this very moment.

I want you to be sure to read through each of the seven deadly fears as we discuss them, even if your gut reaction is that you don't struggle with some of them. You do. Some of our deepest fears are buried beneath layers of junk and are deeply embedded in the recesses of our minds, working against us in surprisingly subtle ways. As we talked about earlier, by not having a strategic life plan or pursuing concrete goals, you may be allowing your unconscious fears to dictate your life in a way that makes you chronically avoid confronting fears you didn't even think you had. Do you reach into a pot of boiling-hot water with your bare hands to grab spaghetti noodles? Of course not. The fear of being burned is already deeply ingrained in the way you think. That fear is real and healthy. It's based on fact, but most fears are based on lies.

We all have deeply embedded psychological fears that cause us to avoid certain aspects of life. These fears, though, are rarely based on concrete, indisputable facts. What this means is that fear is a choice. It's a choice to believe the worst possible predictions of the future. The likelihood of these things happening is slim to none, but what is predictable is that if you live in fear you are basically flushing your own potential down the toilet. Fear is an ugly form of self-sabotage. But before we go into the seven most common fears, let me tell you five disastrous consequences of living in fear:

> **Fear is an ugly form of self-sabotage.**

1. *Missed Opportunities:* If you live in fear you will talk yourself out of one opportunity after another, giving an excuse each time as to why you're not good enough.

2. *A Life Full of Regrets:* When I almost died in the car accident, I was overwhelmed with regrets—not about poor decisions I had made, but about opportunities that I thought I had missed.

3. *Hills Become Mountains:* In life you will encounter real obstacles, but fear has a way of making surmountable hills look and feel like Mount Everest.

4. *Fears Become Phobias:* If you aren't careful, a small unaddressed fear can turn into a full-fledged phobia that cripples your progress in life.

5. *Stunted Growth:* Fear has a way of freezing you in place and not allowing you to grow and mature emotionally in the ways you will need to if you are going to live out your life goals.

THE SEVEN DEADLY FEARS

Fear of Failure—Atychiphobia

Right now, the world is full of people who are getting rich (or at least making a living) off of ideas you had but never pursued. I'm sure you've had it happen before: you have a brilliant flash of an idea that you discard—only to see a company execute some variation of the idea years later. In fact, my guess is that the most ingenious ideas in the history of the world didn't die on last week's episode of *Shark Tank* but instead died in the hearts and minds of those who couldn't push past their fear of failure. It's sad even writing those words when I consider that real cures to what ails our world may be lying dormant, right now, in the minds of people gripped by fear.

The fear of failure is an unhealthy prediction that your ideas and dreams and goals and passions are not truly worth pursuing, because you will probably flop in the end anyway. Rarely is a history of failure what causes the fear to set up shop in our minds— quite the opposite actually. The most successful people in the world fail big and fail often. They hate it, but they don't fear it. Those of us who have actually failed too many times to count have learned what the thought of failure will never tell you—it is never the big, bad bogeyman that you imagine it to be. In fact, some of the most exhilarating moments of my life came as I bounced back from failure.

Remember when I decided to train to climb a mountain when the doctors were advising spinal fusion surgery? When I finally made my way to a punishing six-day mountaineering school on the glaciers ten thousand feet up on Mount Baker in Washington, I pushed my body *way* beyond the limits of what I thought possible. For an entire day we had something called self-arrest training, where our instructors, tasked with teaching us how to save ourselves if we ever lost

The most successful people in the world fail big and fail often.

control and fell down a mountain, did something that is going to sound crazy to you now—they literally held us by our feet on steep icy hills and dropped us so that we could practice the skills we'd learned, like digging our cleats and ice axes into the ground to stop the momentum of our fall. We did it dozens of times, over and over again. Basically, if you didn't stop yourself, you'd tumble all the way to the bottom, ten stories below. Obviously, they set it up so you wouldn't die, but it certainly wasn't cool if you failed. The purpose was to give you the skills you needed in case something should happen. After four brutal days in the mountaineering school, the self-arrest training beat me up so badly that I had to be taken to a hospital six hours away due to pain and exhaustion. However, while I failed to finish, the lessons I learned then not only helped me in life and leadership but showed me that I could push my body harder than I thought possible. Just months prior, the experts had been telling me I had to give up being active and undergo life-altering surgeries. Five years later, I still haven't had to have spinal surgery and rarely have the level of pain that used to stop me in my tracks for weeks on end.

Failure has an uncanny way of teaching you more than you expected while showing you what options you have left in life. A few years ago I hastily sold the first tech company that I ever built. Thinking I was going to still be a part of the team, I was fired from it just a few months later. The company failed soon thereafter, and I felt like I had failed, too. I'm not going to lie—it hurt. It hurt my pride and ego more than anything else, but it also put me in a financial bind. Failure, fundamentally unlike success, causes you to reflect. Backed into a real corner, I was left to reflect on what got me there and what I wanted out of life moving forward. I'm not here to say that I am glad it happened like that, but the lessons I learned from that failure have made my current businesses exponentially stronger. I also learned not to put too much of my self-worth and identity into the work that I do so that my self-esteem isn't dictated by the ups and downs of business success and failure.

I tell you all of this to show you that not starting something because it might fail is basically a failure in and of itself, so you might as well give life a full try. By failing to start, you deprive yourself of ever knowing what could be possible and the invaluable lessons you will learn no matter how the journey goes.

You *can* bounce back from failure. The human mind, body, and soul are resilient. I'm not trying to romanticize failure. I hate failing and want to avoid it like the plague myself, but life has a way of giving us many second chances. Don't obsess over the consequences to the point of having an irrational fear that you will fall apart at the seams if something doesn't work out. When you do fail, as best as you can, learn the lessons you need to learn to avoid failing that same way again, then quickly move on. Don't linger in the failure too long. Don't throw a pity party either. The best quarterbacks in the NFL are those who can throw a terrible interception on a crucial play, then follow that up on the next possession with a confident drive down the field as if the earlier interception were never thrown. Even the very best quarterbacks of all time blow the game occasionally. They just know how to move on.

THREE SIMPLE SOLUTIONS

1. Google "successful people who failed big." It's a who's who of the world.

2. Talk to people on social media or in person about their biggest failures and how they recovered. This will help demystify failure for you and make encountering it far less daunting.

3. Like ancient samurai would do, envision the worst-case scenarios for the biggest risks you are considering. While this may seem counterintuitive, it is an exercise that actually builds up your courage. Furthermore, you can have peace of mind in knowing that the worst-case scenario rarely happens.

Fear of Going Broke—Peniaphobia

Nobody wants to go broke. However, the fear of losing all your money and living in abject poverty is one of the most self-fulfilling fears of them all. The sad truth is that the fear of being broke causes good people to avoid the calculated risks that are necessary to actually build wealth. We conquer the fear of being broke not by dwelling on the fear, but by putting plans in place to ensure it never happens: increasing our earning potential and decreasing our expenses, creating an emergency fund, and investing smartly—particularly in the life goals we'll soon establish together. Sometimes it may be the case that even when you do all of these things, your fear of going broke never quite disappears, but you will not achieve your life goals and maximize your full potential in the world if you don't deal with this head-on.

I can speak on being broke with real authority, and I hope what I'm about to share will give you some comfort. I've been on food stamps in the past. I've had three full-time jobs simultaneously before and worked over 100 hours a week to make ends meet. I know what it's like to be jobless and have to burn through your savings. I know what it's like to be a full-time college student with a family and a full-time job. Having been broke more times than I wished during the course of my life, I've experienced it enough to know that I never want to go back. I've also been broke enough to know that it's not the end of the world. I'm not saying I want to be barely scraping by again, but my wife and kids will tell you to this day that some of the best times of our lives were when all we really had was one another and the bare necessities. When I was a kid I never cared a day in my life about how much square footage our home had or if we had a huge television. But when I got married and had kids, all of a sudden I started acting like those things mattered. They don't. My big family has lived in two of the tiniest apartments in the history of apartments and made some of our most beloved memories in them. To this day when we ask our kids which of the homes we lived in they love the most, they regularly list the smallest and cheapest of them all. They actually preferred the small places, because it meant they were always close to Rai and me. Whatever situation you find yourself in, try to find the blessings and benefits of that moment.

However—and this is key—if you are going to have a fear of being broke, you must choose to let it inspire you to make smart and aggressive decisions instead of causing you to be frozen into inaction—not only with your personal finances, but with your career and your life goals. If you work our plan the right way, it is exceedingly likely that you are going to make more money doing what you love and what brings you happiness than you'll ever make in any job or career that has you praying for the weekend to hurry up and get here. Almost more than any other fear you could ever have, this one has a well-worn path taken by many people who came before you. While their paths and yours will not be perfectly parallel, the way out has similar steps for all of us.

THREE SIMPLE SOLUTIONS

1. Google "famous people who survived bankruptcy." Some of my favorite people ever are on that list.

2. Declare now that you are going to have an airtight financial plan for your life. Dave Ramsey's *The Total Money Makeover* can help get you there.

3. Get serious now about decreasing your spending and increasing your income. I'll make practical suggestions on both later, but commit to this today.

Fear of the Unfamiliar—Xenophobia

No way around it—fear of the unfamiliar has some of the ugliest consequences in life, so much so that the clinical term for this fear, xenophobia, is now widely used around the world when referring to discrimination against immigrants and other ethnic groups by people in power. However, it goes way beyond this.

When you fear what you don't know, you create a prison for yourself. While this prison might not have physical bars, it has emotional ones that can sometimes be even stronger. What makes this particularly sad is that your world becomes puny, and the fear of the unknown locks you into that puny little world. You start exaggerating the quality of what you know and denigrating that which you don't know, putting down the unfamiliar in order to fully justify the consequences of your fear. This is scary, because you give yourself permission to stop growing . . . and if you're not growing, you're dying. People who choose to stop learning, to stop challenging themselves, to stop experiencing new things, are basically saying they know all that they will ever want or need to know. But whether you want to admit it or not, the best lessons and experiences of your life are still ahead of you unless you shut them all down preemptively.

Don't get me wrong, you have a ton to be thankful for in what you *do* already know and have, but understand that outside of your self-imposed prison is a beautiful, colorful, exciting, challenging world—and I'm not just talking about what you find when you take international trips. In your own city are people, places, art, food, music, and even new friends waiting for you to get over yourself and discover what you've been missing.

> **If you're not growing, you're dying.**

THREE SIMPLE SOLUTIONS

1. Try new experiences right away as they present themselves, and focus on practical activities that are outside of your routine. At first this may mean eating new types of food, reading different types of books, or buying different types of music, but eventually it should mean traveling to new places and making new friends.

2. Answer this question: "What have I denied myself because of my fear of the unknown?" Then determine if it has been worth it for you to miss out on these things.

3. Become a serial researcher. Education is the absolute biggest solution to the fear of the unknown, and more information is available to you now than at any point in human history. While I'm willing to jump into something new sooner than most, I never do it without some initial research to get the base level of comfort that I require.

Fear of Being Alone—Monophobia

The fear of being alone is actually very common and has many expressions, ranging from the fear of being apart from a particular person or group of people to the fear of being alone at home, the fear of being alone in public, or even the fear of traveling long distances alone. Mainly rooted in some irrational fear of danger or crisis, the fear of being alone is one that must be addressed if you are going to set and pursue real life goals, because you are inevitably going to have to stand alone in life at some point or another, even if just in the early stages of your most ambitious goals. Your loved ones and friends will not always be able to be there with you, and sometimes they may even disagree with your plans, but you must not let your fear of being alone, literally or figuratively, keep you from moving forward. In fact, it's highly unlikely that you are going to have people around you who understand and appreciate all of the dreams that are on your heart, and if having people around is a requirement for you to pursue those dreams, you're in trouble.

I have known men and women to actually live with people they hate (and who hate them) simply because they'd rather be miserable with company than have some level of peace alone. I've known people who wanted to go to college but opted out because they weren't sure what their uneducated friends would think. I've known people who felt called, deep in their hearts and souls, to make a particular difference in the world but chose to ignore that call because they worried that the people around them would think it was silly. I've known people who even felt like they heard the voice of God whisper to them about making a big move to a new state or a new country, but they chose to ignore that voice rather than risk being alone in an unfamiliar place. I've known people—good people, in fact—who have witnessed horrible atrocities but chose not to say anything, because they just weren't able to muster up the strength to stand alone.

I'm not encouraging you to be a loner, per se, but to embrace the reality that you are going to have to stand alone and be alone from time to time if you are going to experience the fullness of what life has waiting for you. Your losing weight, or getting fit, or learning a new language, or moving to New York City can't rely on someone else's doing it with you.

THREE SIMPLE SOLUTIONS

1. Online friends and support groups can do so much to ease the loneliness of the journey you may be on. One of the most beautiful aspects of social media is that it can connect kindred spirits with very similar affinities who may be thousands of miles apart. Maybe nobody understands you in your zip code, but surely you make sense to someone online.

2. Slowly ease into a solitary activity. You don't even have to tell anyone you're doing it. Take a night class. Join a fitness group full of strangers. Do something as simple as going to see a movie alone to begin addressing this fear and getting more comfortable with yourself.

3. Pay a nonrefundable deposit on something ambitious to do on your own, like climbing a mountain, taking a

humanitarian trip abroad, or taking a personal enrich-
ment course.

Fear of Rejection—Kakorrhaphiophobia

Perhaps more than any other fear, this one robs us of the innocence
and imagination of our youth. Whereas we were once willing to try
new things and have fun no matter the outcome, something about
each year that passed introduced a fear of the rejection, and scorn,
and laughter at our expense when we fail. For some of us, just
one experience of being laughed at or teased was all we needed to
develop a deep fear that has continued well into adulthood. The
truth is, everybody hates to face failure. Within all of us is a desire
to be appreciated and even respected, and few things sting more
than having someone say that something you've poured your heart
into comes up short.

I know this kind of rejection all too well. In fact—and I'm not
even joking here—I am pretty sure my close, enduring lifelong
friendship with failure is what allows me to be rejected over and
over again, but keep on pushing forward. I think I messed up more
in the past two years than the previous ten years combined. Two
years ago I started a new business called Upfront. It was a way for
fans to pay for premium content from the artists and leaders they
admired the most. When we were just getting started, my cofounder
and I both left everything behind to start Upfront. Sometimes we
would have three to four meetings a day where we would pitch our
new app to agents, managers, record labels, film companies, and

artists themselves. Combined we probably had 200 meetings on four continents pitching our app. It was time-consuming, and it was expensive—particularly for a young start-up like ours.

In our 200 meetings, close to 200 people rejected us. Some outright told us we were going to fail, but at least they did it quickly. Others would take four hours to ask eighty-seven questions and then tell us no. I grew to like the ones who said no right away. It was hard, and a huge part of the struggle was that you had to approach meeting 124 with real enthusiasm—even though you had just been rejected 123 times. It was because we endured rejection over and over again that we eventually found people who dug what we were doing and wanted to support the company either with an investment or with talent. In our 200 meetings over the course of a year, the five or six people who told us yes were all we needed to stay alive.

Every person you admire in history has had to endure severe rejection at one time or another on their path to success. Their ability to endure and overcome is some of what you love about them. In sports, few stories are ever as popular as that of the star athlete who was once passed over by every team in the draft before becoming a champion. In business, the stories that get told over and over again are rarely ones of long, uninterrupted success, but the ones of innovators who were told time and time again that their idea was terrible before it finally became a runaway success. Even if people don't believe in you now, one day your results will speak for themselves.

THREE SIMPLE SOLUTIONS

1. Flip the way you view rejection. It's very, very easy when you are rejected to get down on yourself, but you must learn that when someone rejects you, it says way more about them than it does about you. It's when you internalize how other people feel about you and make it how you feel about yourself that it becomes a problem.

2. Google "famous rejection letters," and see the actual rejection letters sent to some of the most famous authors and artists and musicians in history.

3. Get rejected more. While it's true that the more you put your ideas out there, the more you may be rejected, you will also build up immunity to it over time. My best advice here is to have zero expectations that people are going to love (or even like) your idea when you present it to them. Know that what makes perfect sense in your mind—because you've thought about it and mulled it over 100 times—may take just as long for others to understand. This is particularly true for family members. If you share an idea or goal with them, do not expect them to believe in it as much as you do. This way, if they do love it, it's just a bonus.

Fear of Death—Thanatophobia

Probably the most complicated fear in the world is the fear of death. In fact, because it can only happen once in a person's life and because we don't have sufficient firsthand reports of what happens after we die, some psychologists say that none of us actually fear death but fear other things like pain, how we may die, the unknown world beyond death, loss of control, leaving behind relatives, and the disappointment of an incomplete life. Either way, when you have a real fear of death or the things leading up to it or caused by it, the most common side effect is a life lived without risk.

I'm not ready to die. I have four kids, a wife I'm crazy about, and many unfulfilled goals and dreams. I'd like to live a long, healthy life if possible, but I've come close enough to death to know that it could happen to any of us tomorrow and wasting time worrying about it is utterly counterproductive.

Recently, an experienced hospice-care nurse revealed that she had been taking notes for years from her patients in their last days on earth. Without fail, over and over again, the patients expressed to her five regrets:

1. They regretted working too much, which caused them to miss precious time with family.

2. They regretted not speaking their mind more often when they had a chance to do so.

3. They regretted not pursuing their own goals and dreams instead of conforming to others' expectations.

4. They wished they'd let themselves be happier in life.

5. They wished they'd stayed in better touch with friends and family.

When I first read those five regrets, I was truly stung, because I was already having some of them myself. Maybe some of them ring true to you, too, but what I know is this: living life in fear of death is a strange waste of time. We know it's coming. We know our time is ever so finite. We know we have little time to waste, yet we spend so much of our time on the mundane when most people, in their last days, wish they'd lived more loudly and openly and deliberately. Let's truly live our best lives while we have the time to do so, okay?

THREE SIMPLE SOLUTIONS

1. Search YouTube for "Randy Pausch last lecture," and watch this beloved professor facing a terminal illness speak about what it really means to live! Pausch's book *The Last Lecture* is also spectacular.

2. Reread the five regrets of the dying, and ask yourself if your fear of death is causing you to live a life that will leave you with those regrets yourself.

3. Do some basic things like making a will and purchasing a huge life insurance policy to give you more peace of mind about what will happen after you pass away.

Fear of Public Speaking—Glossophobia

In so many ways, the fear of public speaking is huge, because it combines so many other fears, like the fear of failure, the fear of rejection, and even the fear of being alone all into one big public moment. Indeed, almost nobody is afraid of speaking; it's the public part, in front of a crowd, that freaks people out all over the world. You may want to dismiss this fear as being irrelevant to you, but please stay with me. I am almost completely certain that at least a few of your 100 life goals will require you to speak before some type of crowd, large or small. You may not need to be the keynote speaker for a conference, but if you ever need investors to fund your business or a publisher to believe in your book or Congress to listen to your testimony or the president of the company you work for to buy into your innovative idea, you are going to need to know how to speak comfortably in front of a crowd.

About two years ago I was asked to fill in and speak three times on a Sunday morning for a pastor at the height of his popularity. It was a huge church used to hearing a great speaker; I was simultaneously honored and nervous. I've been speaking publicly in front of large crowds since I was seventeen years old, so I had plenty of experience. But I hadn't spoken three times in one morning in quite some time. And I have this weird thing where I don't like to eat anything beforehand. The last thing you want as a public speaker is to have to rush to the bathroom in a pinch. In spite of having spoken publicly thousands of times, I still get a bit nervous, and a big meal doesn't help.

Let me tell you the good news first, okay? The two earlier services that Sunday were two of the best speaking experiences of my life. They honestly couldn't have gone any better. People loved and understood my message; they laughed at my jokes and connected with my stories. But two things fell apart for me when it came time to speak at the third service. First, I didn't know it then, but I had gone too long without eating or drinking. I just wasn't sharp. My mind was hazy, and I had poured too much out without giving my body any fuel. Second, when you speak three times in one day, it can be hard to say the same jokes with the same stories and the same points again. It's not that it's insincere, but it kind of feels like it and it threw me off a bit.

Long story short, I bombed. I mean majorly. Like bad on an epic level. Nobody laughed at my jokes. My thoughts were jumbled. My message and points were unclear. It was an all-around socially awkward encounter. I kid you not, while I was speaking I daydreamed of a trapdoor underneath the podium that I so badly hoped would open up and suck me somewhere deep into the earth. I wanted to disappear! It was that bad. To make matters worse, my wife had traveled with me, so she was there to witness this debacle and we carried the shame back home with us.

You are probably wondering when I am going to make you feel better about public speaking.

The next day—heck, by later that night—I was over it. I had spoken well the two other times, I've spoken well most of my life, and I bombed once. Nobody threw tomatoes at me. It wasn't a trending topic on Twitter. I wasn't arrested. I was just bad for forty-five minutes, and the world moved on. If your worst nightmare happens and you bomb like I did, your life will also go on!

THREE SIMPLE SOLUTIONS

1. Speak in your own voice like you do when you are talking in a conversation with friends and family. This immediately gets your mind off the fear of having to sound like somebody you aren't.

2. Prepare as far in advance and as much as you can. I don't memorize my speeches word for word, but I do memorize the key points I am going to make so that I can sound as natural and confident as possible. I have friends who memorize every word, but I just don't have that skill.

3. Rehearse important speeches by delivering them in front of friends and family, or on camera, so you can play them back. Before people speak on the main stage of TED they have to do this many, many times in front of the producers to make sure it's just right.

DIG IN

Now that we've identified the seven biggest fears, don't just let them be words on the page for someone else to consider. Dig into them, consider the simple solutions I've provided, and even search out solutions of your own. Which of the seven fears do you struggle with most? Do you feel like any of your fears have grown into full-fledged phobias? How have these fears impacted your life? How have they gotten in the way of your dreams and goals? How have

they inhibited your growth? Answering these questions and properly confronting your fears will not only allow you to have good
momentum as you launch into your 100 life goals, but it will help
you avoid or even leapfrog past roadblocks that have derailed you
in the past.

Money is not required to buy one necessity of the soul.

—HENRY DAVID THOREAU

Money is only a tool. It will take you wherever you wish,
but it will not replace you as the driver.

—AYN RAND

Wealth flows from energy and ideas.

—WILLIAM FEATHER

Too many people spend money they haven't earned, to buy
things they don't want, to impress people they don't like.

—WILL ROGERS

3

IF MONEY WASN'T A PROBLEM

Starting Where You Are and Believing You Will Have Enough

While fear is the biggest internal obstacle keeping you from living your best life, no external excuse is used more often to explain away mediocrity than the idea that you can't afford anything else. That we'd do so much more in life if only we had more money might be the biggest, most consistent lie told around the world. Sadly, and somewhat strangely, it's a lie that doesn't go away even when you make the money that you thought would give you the courage and opportunity to live out your dreams. More times than not, courage, passion, determination, and focus are what ultimately produce money. It's rarely the other way around. Waiting to have a certain amount of money before you start living your best life is like chasing a mirage in the desert.

I've seen it over and over again. When you are dead broke, living paycheck to paycheck, on the verge of homelessness, you imagine how much differently (and boldly) you are going to live life when you make more money. You tell yourself that you will be more charitable and that the dreams and witty ideas you've been delaying will finally come to fruition. But when you get a raise or a new, better-paying job, instead of pursuing your life goals, you simply live a slightly cushier version of your previous life. Your rent goes up, your TV gets a little bigger, your groceries get a little better, you go from Dell to Apple products, you eat out a little more, you join the local health club, and instead of radically changing your world—or anyone else's, for that matter—you make a new world that looks pretty much just like your old world, only with a few more name brands. I've been there, done that, gotten the T-shirt and bumper sticker.

> Waiting to have a certain amount of money before you start living your best life is like chasing a mirage in the desert.

Most people all over the world, ranging from those living in the impoverished townships of South Africa to those in the exclusive high-rises of Manhattan, feel like they can't afford to act on their dreams. Indeed, the men and women whom I've met in South Africa could never believe, in their wildest imaginations, that the men and women living on the forty-first floor of an expensive New York City apartment building, while their quality of life may be better, actually have almost no extra money at the end of the month to pursue their dreams either.

Without going all deep or philosophical on you, I want to suggest that the consumer systems of the world thrive on your eating, drinking, wearing, clicking, and shopping your life away. Corporations are counting on you to increase your cost of living with every little income bump you receive. Of course, none of them are going to come out and say they want you to flush your dreams down the toilet to buy their shiny new gadgets, but this is our reality, and it will continue to be your reality unless you start where you are right now and decide that you are the one who will tell your money what to do and how to fund your goals.

WHY COLLEGE DROPOUTS ARE SUCH GREAT STARTERS

Peter Thiel, the cofounder of PayPal and the first outside investor in Facebook (he ended up with a whopping 10 percent of the company), saw with his own eyes (and money) what Mark Zuckerberg, a college dropout, could build. In fact, Thiel, himself a Stanford-educated attorney by trade, was so convinced that college dropouts have some type of secret sauce that he recently started a fellowship that pays the smartest college students with the best ideas $100,000 to drop out and pursue them. When he first announced the idea, academia was outraged, but even a quick glance at the accomplishments of college dropouts would make a hard-core skeptic change their mind.

Two decades before Mark Zuckerberg and friends dropped out of Harvard, a free-spirited California hippie and tech whiz, Steve Jobs, dropped out of college. Soon thereafter he teamed up with Steve Wozniak, also a college dropout, and they built some of the best personal computers ever designed at that time—which became the foundation of Apple.

Around the same time, Paul Allen, a young computer expert who had a perfect score on the SAT, dropped out of college and began asking his friend Bill Gates to do the same. Together they built Microsoft. Gates is now the second richest man in the world. Sadly, Paul Allen is just the fifty-fifth richest and only owns three professional sports teams, including the Seattle Seahawks and the Portland Trail Blazers.

Larry Ellison, now the fifth richest man in the world, dropped out of college to pursue a career in technology after just one semester. He soon founded Oracle, whose hardware and software are the backbone of the Internet.

It's not just technological geniuses who dropped out of college to pursue their dreams, though. Oprah Winfrey dropped out to become a news broadcaster. Ellen DeGeneres dropped out to pursue comedy. Tom Hanks dropped out to pursue acting. David Geffen dropped out to pursue a career as an executive in the music industry.

In fact, I had a real 360-degree moment in writing this chapter. A few weeks after I learned that Oprah Winfrey, Larry Ellison, and David Geffen had all dropped out of college, they came together to express their interest in purchasing the Los Angeles Clippers NBA franchise. I could go on and on and on here. When you get a chance, Google "famous college dropouts" for yourself to see how amazing the list is. It spans every generation and every industry, but why?

College students may have 1,001 good things going for them, but money is rarely one. In fact, college students are notoriously broke, but what they lack in money they make up for in courage. Furthermore, they are in a unique stage of life where they rarely have a family, can live like slobs, and can work twenty-four focused hours a day with little regard for the relational consequences. College dropouts are particularly determined, focused, and fearless, because they are keenly aware that they are abandoning their safety nets to pursue their passions.

I am certainly not advocating that college students, en masse, drop out to follow their dreams or that those of you who have already finished should go back and try dropping out for a change! However, I do think successful college dropouts can teach us three transferrable principles no matter what life stage you currently find yourself in.

1. *You have to believe in your vision for the future enough to make other people think you're crazy.* The successful people I just named believed enough in the merit of their own ideas to forsake convention, tradition, and the societal pressure to finish school. It took guts for each and every one of them to believe enough in the relatively invisible possibility of big success to trade the moderate guarantees given by a college degree for that possibility.

2. *You have to take a risk big enough that failing could really cost you something.* Each of the examples above had invested real time and money into college when they decided to drop out. They decided, though, that they'd rather give their dreams a try and fail than always wonder what could have been. I truly think the added pressure gives them that extra push to succeed that is too often lacking in society as a whole.

3. *You have to put real time into your dreams and goals.* Successful college dropouts, and scores like them, could have succeeded in college, but succeeding in college meant they wouldn't have had enough time to pursue their passions. Sometimes you have to quit things that matter to devote the necessary time to go after things that will ultimately matter much more.

Consider that you have as much money today as Oprah Winfrey or Tom Hanks did when they dropped out of college and did the hard work of making their dreams come true. In other words, you have all of the money you need to get started—even if you're broke. Here's why . . .

THE FIRST THREE STEPS ARE *FREE*!

It's very easy to be intimidated by the size, scope, and cost of your dreams. Sadly, it's when kids become young adults and start understanding the true cost of their childhood dreams that they begin letting go of them completely. They look at the final price tag and rule themselves out of contention before they ever get started.

> Sometimes you have to quit things that matter to devote the necessary time to go after things that will ultimately matter much more.

This is such an awful tragedy, because at least the first three steps to virtually every life goal you could have are completely and totally free. Sometimes, an entire life goal can be achieved for free, but, without fail, the first steps are *always* free! True, it might cost $300,000 to go to med school nowadays and you only have $419 in your checking account, but nobody who goes to med school has $300,000 in their checking account. I can name three people off the top of my head right now who got into med school with less than $419 in their account! Never allow the total end cost of a goal to make you punk out of pursuing it. Rarely will you pay for an entire goal all at once, and the twenty-seven different doors you need to open for the goal to be attainable will never open up all at once either. Dreams come in stages, and the earliest are almost always the most affordable.

Step #1: Make Up Your Mind!

I'm sorry if this sounds so simple that it's stupid. I assure you it isn't. If you skip this step, it will undermine everything else you do later and make it exponentially more likely that you will throw in the towel long before you should. A clear, focused, determined, made-up mind is your greatest asset as you jump headfirst into pursuing your goals. Sure, having more money might allow you to take a few shortcuts here and there, but a made-up mind will keep your life on mission when you are thrown the inevitable curveballs destined to come your way. By the time I've made up my mind that I'm going to do something, to me it's as good as done. I know you might not feel like that just yet, but as you start crafting your life goals, it's going to be essential that you make time to take this absolutely free step.

If your mind is made up to become debt-free, that's a game changer. At the point when you decide to become a pediatrician, your whole world has changed. When you make up your mind to write your first novel, your life will never be the same again. If you are married, this is a step usually shared with your spouse.

Step #2: Start Free Research and Training!

The Internet and public libraries are beautiful things. After you've truly committed to pursuing a particular goal, I encourage you to jump headfirst into that topic. Become an expert on it. Read every blog out there discussing it. Subscribe to those blogs. Start your own blog about it. Follow every single leader from that field on Twitter, Facebook, and Instagram. Message them, and see if they respond. Subscribe to their e-mail newsletters. Google every relevant topic and keyword about that goal every chance you get. Do it on your lunch break. Check out every leading book on the topic from the public library—then actually read those books. Search out free training videos on YouTube, and watch them from start to finish. Go to the Web pages for experts on the topic, find their contact information, then call or e-mail their offices to ask what free training materials they recommend or if they have any samples they can send you. Get obsessed with it.

As I'm writing this I am living in Cape Town, South Africa. It's long been a dream of mine to one day own a professional sports team. In my mind that team has always been an American sports team, but since I've been here I've become obsessed with South African soccer (yes, they call it football, but I can't make that leap just yet). In the past two months I've pretty much done all of the things I suggested to you above, because I'm dreaming of the possibility of one day owning a successful professional soccer team here. My wife thinks I'm a lunatic (she's probably right), but I can't quit thinking about it. I'm not saying that I know enough to own a team tomorrow, but I know enough to know it'd be a blast.

While you could earnestly conduct research on any particular topic for months or years, don't get stuck in this stage. Remember that you are conducting this research to give you confidence for what's next. Also, if you haven't noticed, we still haven't spent any money yet.

Step #3: Start Your Engine!

After you've made up your mind to pursue a particular life goal and have become obsessed with free research and training about it, now is the time to start your engine. Let me be very specific about what I mean here. Starting the engine of a car is not the same as backing it out of your driveway, and it's certainly not the same as driving it full speed down the highway. However, starting an engine requires you to have the car in working order, with the keys in your hand and your butt in the driver's seat. When you start the engine, all of that free training and research you've been doing is going to come to the front of your mind, and you are going to want to take off on your own . . . but it's not time yet!

Starting your engine is a calculated moment where you go public with your goal. It can be online, it can be with family and friends, or it can just be with the people you may be working with to achieve the goal, but this is the point in time where the idea goes from a secret in your head to something other people become aware of. It doesn't have to be an overzealous declaration of, "I'm going to climb to the top of Mount Everest next weekend," but it can be something like, "I've developed a real love for mountaineering. Been dreaming about it for years. I'm taking my first class next month." Privately, you may know that it's all leading up to your dream of climbing to the top of Mount Everest in three years, but you don't have to go there publicly just yet.

Now let's take a look at some examples of what these three free steps would look like for different life goals.

LIFE GOAL: BE COMPLETELY DEBT-FREE BY JANUARY 1, 2020

- Step 1: Think long and hard about the sacrifices and adjustments needed, but make a firm decision to be rid of every single debt I have, including student loans, by January 1, 2020.

- Step 2: Devour everything written and spoken by Dave Ramsey and Clark Howard without spending a dime in the process, including podcasts, blogs, library books, and more. Ask them and their staff relevant questions by e-mailing them, calling in to their shows, or tweeting at them. Join free online support groups and message boards for people who are on the same journey.

- Step 3: Craft a hard-core budget and set a real timeline based on what I learned from my free mentors and online peers. Make it known to family, friends, and peers that I am about to start on the path to financial freedom.

LIFE GOAL: FINISH ONE OF MY TOP FIVE MED SCHOOL CHOICES IN TEN YEARS OR FEWER

▓ Step 1: Decide and fully accept that the next ten years of my life are going to be almost completely focused on preparing to get into med school, applying for med school, then attending and completing med school.

▓ Step 2: Attend every free med school admissions seminar within 100 miles of my home. Read every book in the public library about choosing schools, med schools, admissions, the MCAT, test prep, and more. Begin taking free mock MCAT tests over and over again. Watch MCAT test prep videos on YouTube. Submit my contact information to the admissions offices of the top med schools I've pinpointed, so I can begin really making my decision on which schools to apply to.

▓ Step 3: Make it known to my close friends and family that I am going to med school and that I am about to make getting into a top school my only hobby for the next twelve months.

LIFE GOAL: PUBLISH TWO NOVELS FROM AN ACTION SERIES FOR KIDS BY SEPTEMBER 17, 2020

▓Step 1: Decide that I am an author. I'm not a guy who dreams of writing; I am a writer. It's in me, and I am going to write and publish the first two books in the teenage action series I've been dreaming of.

Step 2: Read every book on writing and publishing at my local public library. Reread every book that is beloved in the genre, and take notes on what they do well. Subscribe to blogs for writers and newsletters for those who want to be published. Read everything I can about the value of self-publishing versus going with a traditional publisher. Follow all of my favorite authors and publishers on Twitter and Facebook. Audit a creative writing course at my local community college.

Step 3: Begin making notes and working on outlines for my action series. Make it known to the online writing communities I've joined that I'm finally about to start writing my first book.

STARTING FROM THE BOTTOM

It's easy to assume, when you don't have much money to pursue your dreams and goals, that money is the missing ingredient in your inevitable success. I'm not here to say that throwing some money at your problems won't make them a little easier to handle from time to time, but money is never a magic bullet. A few of the men and women I've grown to really admire not only started out being dead broke but weren't given many breaks from the powers that be either.

Money is never a magic bullet.

I absolutely love the story of Guy Laliberté. A struggling, home-less street performer in Quebec, Canada, Guy was known as a juggler and a pretty impressive fire breather. He loved his work and dreamed of a bigger audience, but it just didn't make him enough to pay the bills. He was forced to take a factory job at a hydro-power plant, and it seemed like Guy was going to have to let go of his dreams. However, the power plant shut down just days after he started working there. Guy took that as a sign from God that he was supposed to live out his dreams. What at first looked like a raw deal forced Guy back into his street performances. After he put together a wacky, colorful group of performers, the troupe built a bit of local momentum. They decided that Los Angeles was a city where they could really succeed. Guy had enough money to get the troupe to Los Angeles but not enough to get them back home to Canada unless they were a rousing success. On that trip alone, they had sixteen sold-out shows and made over $2 million. That troupe, Cirque du Soleil, is now the most successful circus of the modern era and employs over four thousand people around the world.

Her mother had recently died. She was unemployed. Her marriage had just ended in a bitter divorce. She was on welfare and had a restraining order filed against her abusive ex-husband. In the midst of all this, J. K. Rowling, a single mom, wrote her first Harry Potter book. She was turned down by the first twelve publishers she submitted to. I won't even bother telling you what happened next. I'm sure you've heard that her books became a pretty big deal.

Selling fax machines door-to-door in the Florida heat, Sara Blakely knew in her heart that she could design a much better pair of panty hose than what was out there for women wearing open-toed shoes. Armed only with her idea and several business books she bought at Barnes & Noble, Blakely successfully filed and received a patent for her uniquely designed control-top panty hose. However, she couldn't find even a single factory willing to produce them for her, and she was planning to pay for them herself! But with her company Spanx, Sara Blakely eventually became the youngest female self-made billionaire in the world and the first woman to join Warren Buffett and Bill Gates to pledge to give away at least half of her wealth in her lifetime.

Beaten regularly by his father and molested by a neighbor, Tyler Perry attempted suicide more than once as a teenager to escape the horrible pain he faced. As an adult he regularly lived in his car while self-financing a one-man stage play he hoped to get off the ground. It took years and years of performing his plays all over the United States before his work truly caught on. Just recently Tyler Perry was listed by *Forbes* magazine as the highest-paid entertainer in the world.

Stephen King, possibly one of the most successful authors in the history of the world, struggled mightily to provide for his young family before anything he wrote became a blockbuster success. An unemployed twenty-two-year-old dad, Stephen King took a job at an industrial Laundromat to make ends meet. His short horror stories were being rejected by publishers and magazines way more than they were being accepted. Barely getting by, he was living in a dumpy trailer when his wife encouraged King to throw himself into writing his first real novel, *Carrie*. He was elated when a publisher gave him a $2,500 advance for the book. Once published, it became such an enormous hit among readers that he was given $400,000 just a few months later for the paperback publishing rights.

Wherever you are in life, whatever you are up against now or have had to overcome in the past, the fact that you are alive is a sign that you have much more to do and accomplish on this earth. The key is going to be to just start. The amount of money you have may determine a few steps in your strategic plan, but it shouldn't impact whether or not you actually start working toward your dreams and goals. While everybody may think that all the people I listed in this chapter are special somehow, folks sure didn't think that when those same people were at the bottom working their way up. Even if you only have one, you already have every single penny you need to get started!

I've only just a minute,

Only sixty seconds in it.

Forced upon me, can't refuse it,

Didn't seek it, didn't choose it,

But it's up to me to use it.

I must suffer if I lose it,

Give an account if I abuse it,

Just a tiny little minute,

But eternity is in it.

—DR. BENJAMIN E. MAYS

Time is a created thing. To say "I don't have time,"

is like saying, "I don't want to."

—LAO TZU

4

IF YOU HAD MORE TIME

*Cutting the Trivial from Your Daily Life
and Maximizing Every Spare Moment*

The shortest month of the year has 672 hours.

I'm not about to tell you how many hours you need to sleep, eat, bathe, and fart. It's just not my style. However, I *am* going to ask that you carve out a minimum of 45 hours a month exclusively for the pursuit of the life goals that we will soon develop together. I'd honestly rather you give closer to 100 hours, but let's start with 45. That means that even in February you will have 627 hours left to do your thing. While it's true that your dreams will get accomplished through the daily details you get done, I want you to take a moment with me to do something that you should do as often as possible: let's take a macro look at your life. Let's pull away, for a few moments, from the chores you have, the bills that are due, and the e-mails you have to reply to. They'll be there waiting for you in a few minutes when you finish this chapter.

A year has 8,766 hours.

A decade, obviously, has ten times that with 87,660 hours.

If you live to be seventy years old, which is now slightly below average, you will live a whopping 613,620 hours of life on this earth.

That is a *huge* amount of time, and it's likely that you'll have even more than that to work with. I'll be honest with you—before I made these calculations, I was thinking we had far less time. I literally had to double- and triple-check my math to make sure the numbers were correct. Here's what is so amazingly fascinating about that reality. I believe that Malcolm Gladwell's observation is correct. It takes about 10,000 hours of dutiful practice and experience in a particular field to become a master in it. The thing is, though, when we hear that it takes 10,000 hours to become a master in something, I don't think we realize that 10,000 hours is but a drop in the bucket of our lives.

When I saw that it's likely we'll have 613,620 hours or more on earth, three immediate thoughts came to my mind:

1. *How many hours have I already been alive?* My age (35 years) x 8,766 hours = 306,810 hours! I couldn't believe it. The good news is that I likely have that many more hours ahead of me, but I must admit that when I see I've already spent 306,810 hours on earth, I can't help but wonder if I could have used at least 10,000 of them to become a master at something unique—like French cuisine, or the martial art of Brazilian jiujitsu, or a foreign language that would allow me to seamlessly weave in and out of another culture.

2. If it's true that I am going to be sleeping for 100,000 of the approximately 300,000 hours I have left, shouldn't I make sure that I am a master of sleep and that it's as beautiful and restful as possible? How could I be so bad at something I spend so much time doing?

3. How can I immediately begin planning to use the 300,000 or so hours that I likely have left in a way that's meaningful and impactful for my family, myself, and the world? Could I strategically carve out 10 percent of that time to become a master of three new skills or practices?

As you move forward in this book, and in life, I want you to develop the ability to toggle back and forth between the two lives that you lead. One life is lived minute by minute. It is your present reality. It is often stressful, unpredictable, and is sometimes boring. The other life is the macro life that your daily life will add up to.

Follow me for a second. I'd like for us to perform a visualization exercise together.

Imagine a painting about the height and width of a bedroom pillow. It's lying flat on a long coffee table made of dark bamboo. It's a beautiful portrait of the sun setting over the ocean. Somehow the sky and clouds have a pinkish-red hue to them but have cast a rainbow of colors over the now-glowing water. Your mind drifts to the many sunsets you've seen with your own eyes, and you realize that you have witnessed a sunset very similar to the one in this painting. You reach down to pick it up. It's not a painting, but it's the cover to a large puzzle box. When you lift it up, the lid to the box comes off and reveals what looks like 1,000 small puzzle pieces—each the size of your thumbnail. You recognize the pinks and reds and blues on the puzzle pieces from the artwork on the lid. You reach your hand down into the box, grab a handful of them—like little bits of the sun and sky and ocean in your hand—and let them fall through your fingers back into the box. At that moment, you decide that you will build and organize those 1,000 pieces into the artwork displayed on the cover. It may take you a month, maybe two, but it is your new mission. For now, you grab the cover and slide it back over the top of the box and are thankful for the wonderful gift that is now yours to assemble.

I'd like for you to begin seeing every day of your life not just as a random set of mundane requirements and activities to slog through, but as a puzzle piece, one small puzzle piece, in a large, brightly colored artistic wonder. Some days the puzzle piece will be a random slice of the sky, and it will be nearly impossible to see how that random piece will ever fit in with the other 200 pieces just like it. Other days it will be like one of the four magical corners to the puzzle. You will know exactly what it means and where it goes, and life, for that moment, will all make

> **Each piece of the puzzle plays its part, and while some pieces seem so much more important than others, they are all required to form your life.**

sense. Cherish those days. More than anything, though, know that each and every hour of each and every day matters. Each piece of the puzzle plays its part, and while some pieces seem so much more important than others, they are all required to form your life. Some days will be cloudy, others will be full of sun, but they will all come together to form your beautiful life.

Now, knowing that you likely have hundreds of thousands of

hours remaining in life, let's really dig into how you can maximize those hours to accomplish your dreams and goals.

FORTY-FIVE HOURS A MONTH

Now, as in right now, I'd like for you to begin thinking of how you could devote a minimum of forty-five hours a month to pursuing your 100 life goals. We'll crank that time up every chance we get, but let's start at forty-five. Depending on your daily schedule and the demands on your time, you may choose to do forty-five minutes in the morning and thirty minutes at night every day of the week. You may devote six hours on Saturday and six on Sunday. You may be so slammed in life right now that you have to find fifteen minutes here and fifteen minutes there until life settles down. Whatever you have to do, it's essential that you decide right now to devote an average of about eleven hours a week to this. Remember, the shortest month of the year has 672 hours, and other months hop up to 744 hours. You can afford forty-five hours a month for crafting and pursuing your 100 life goals. Don't allow this to stress you out either. I'm not asking you to cram yet one more thing into your daily schedule. I am asking you to begin being deliberate and purposeful about how you spend your time and live your life.

Over ten years ago I read a small book called *Choosing to Cheat* by Andy Stanley. It changed my life forever. In it, Andy observed that the modern person is being pulled forcefully in more directions than ever before. It's nearly impossible to avoid, and someone is always going to feel like they are being cheated by you. If you don't choose who and what are going to feel cheated, the choice is going to be made *for* you. Period. And when you don't choose who or what gets cheated, it will always be you, your self-care, and your family that get cheated. You must make deliberate, counter-cultural decisions to cheat the nonessential elements of your life instead. Instead of choosing to be a master of the nonessentials and an amateur in the essentials (family, health, wholeness), you must begin flipping the script one decision at a time. Your decision to have forty-five hours a month focused on your goals—which include family, finances, health, and more—will be one of the best decisions you've ever made.

TOP SEVEN TIME WASTERS

Over the past four years I've lived in Atlanta, Southern California, New York City, Kentucky, and Cape Town, South Africa. While each of those places is uniquely different, I've found that the same seven time wasters eat away at productivity and cause time bleeds all over the world, across all age groups and economic classes. It's these seven time wasters that cause us to wonder, after seeing we've been alive for hundreds of thousands of hours, where all the time has gone. Your ability to honestly assess how these (or other) time wasters impact your life and to pivot away from these behaviors is one of the best predictors of how successful you'll be at achieving your life goals.

Time Waster #1: Television

This includes Netflix, HBO GO, sports, cable, satellite, downloads, and every other form of you looking at a screen—including phones, tablets, flat-screens, desktops, laptops, and more. The number of hours per week people spend watching a screen is increasing annually. In fact, most of us are 10,000-hour masters at this activity. Heck, some of us are Jedi knights at watching television.

THREE SIMPLE SOLUTIONS

1. You and your family should only allow screen time for one hour a day or less. Some families only allow it on weekends. Whatever rule you set here, give it a schedule and set real parameters. Otherwise you'll find yourself spending 100 hours a month or more doing it. I know a guy who chose to cut out watching football for an entire year and instead grew an amazing business and wrote a book with the time he saved.

2. Cut the number of services you pay for monthly in this area. This will also allow you more money to pursue your goals. If you regularly pay too much, you feel obligated to watch more because you've spent so much money on it.

3. Don't allow so many screens to be used for noneducational purposes all over the house. Many studies speak on how unhealthy it is to have a TV in the bedroom. As parents, for instance, we don't allow our kids to have screen time out of sight or in their rooms. When they are on the

computers, we have constructive activities for them in place of online television shows.

Time Waster #2: Social Media

This includes checking Twitter, Facebook, Instagram, Vine, Google+, dating networks, Pinterest, and every other form of social media. Listen, I've made a living on social media, so this one can be hard for me, too, but it is eating into our productivity like never before and must be addressed.

THREE SIMPLE SOLUTIONS

1. Consider removing social media from your phone and tablet altogether. On your phone and tablet, at least move the icons to the second screen, and turn off all automatic notifications. This I learned from a highly productive leader, and it has helped me stay focused.

2. Only check social media during set times of the day, or make certain times of the day social media–free zones. My wife and I do this, for instance, during our dates, and I have to do this during my focused times of writing or teaching.

3. Follow more people who are truly informative or motivational, and unfollow people who are negative or smutty. I regularly audit who and what I follow and reduce the number every few months to keep me focused and waste less time.

Time Waster #3: Web Surfing

This includes surfing on your phone, tablet, desktop, laptop, or any other device you may use to look at news, gossip, random YouTube videos, shopping sites, or more. What starts out as a Google search can easily turn into a time-wasting tornado if you aren't careful. Try to see the Web as a resource you use to advance your goals instead of an abyss that drains valuable time and energy from your life.

THREE SIMPLE SOLUTIONS

1. Like other time wasters, this one can be sectioned off by creating sacred times where you restrict Web surfing.

2. Consider limiting your online news to one or two sources to prevent meandering.

3. Block any sites that are a personal problem for you or your family, and consider additional software to limit these sites. Also, agree to never delete the browser history so that all of your site visits are available to your family or account-ability partners.

Time Waster #4: Commuting

Brutally long commutes are a fact of life all over the world. I recently met a struggling single mother here in South Africa who travels three hours each way to and from work. While this cannot always be avoided, long commutes are a critical way we lose valuable time to pursue our goals.

THREE SIMPLE SOLUTIONS

1. Do everything you can to lessen the total time and expense of your commute. Every study about commutes shows they're bad for your health, relationships, budget, and more. My family will be moving back to California soon, and we've made the hard decision to live in an area we like a little less in order to not have commuting issues every day.

2. This is one of my biggest life hacks: use the time during your commute wisely. With the money you save from cutting your TV plan down, subscribe to Audible.com, download the app, and listen to top audiobooks during your commute. Audible even allows you to return books you don't like at no cost. You could learn new skills or new languages, and use this time to advance your life in powerful ways if you choose to. Your local library will also have a rich collection of audiobooks for you to check out for free.

3. Leave stressful and negative radio shows alone. A commute is hard enough as it is without having shock jocks telling you that the world is going to hell in a handbasket every seven minutes. It'd be better for you to drive in silence than listen to this poison. It's bad for your health and gives you a negative impression of people and the world. Those hosts don't accurately represent things either and are deliberately attempting to rile you and others up for ratings. Don't fall for it.

Time Waster #5: E-mail

E-mail is completely out of hand nowadays. Beyond the reality that we are overwhelmed with spam and trash, we are also largely allowing personal and work-related e-mail to dictate the flow, pace, and mood of our days.

THREE SIMPLE SOLUTIONS

1. Several of my mentors have removed all automatic notifications of e-mail from every device they own and moved the e-mail icon to the second screen of their phones. I have done the same thing, and I will admit it felt like death at first. I couldn't explain it until I realized that I was addicted to my e-mail. It has been my constant companion for the past fifteen years, and I didn't know what to do when I looked down at my phone and did not see it there. I now have to click on the icon for it to update, don't get any audio or visual notifications, and choose to check it only when I have spare time.

2. You must do the hard work of organizing your e-mail inbox in a way that is efficient and productive. Begin using the filters and folders that come with your free e-mail system. This has to be kept up regularly and will require you to unsubscribe from all newsletters and spam manually or by using a third-party service. The fastest, most thorough way to remove spam and junk for free is through a service called Unroll.Me (www.unroll.me). Do it now.

3. Use the e-mail reply and filing system suggested by David Allen in his classic book *Getting Things Done*. This system has revolutionized my personal and professional communication systems online and will do the same for you.

Time Waster #6: Texting

This includes traditional text messaging and new apps like WhatsApp, Snapchat, Facebook Messenger, and any other way to message back and forth with people. The younger you are, the more likely this is to be a huge time and focus drain for you versus e-mail. Some people are actually sending thousands of messages a day in dozens of simultaneous conversations. While I admire the sense of connection, it won't get you any closer to achieving your 100 life goals.

THREE SIMPLE SOLUTIONS

1. Turn your phone completely off, and put it in a different room or in your bag during the times of day when you need to focus the most. Don't panic; we have lived that way for 99.9 percent of human history.

2. Like I've suggested with other tech addictions, make up your mind that you will only reply to texts and messages during certain hours of the day. I think of these as my online office hours. People don't even need to know you have them. After a while people will get that you have a schedule, or you can come out and tell them.

3. Commit to the idea that you will not use your messages to put any negativity or gossip into the world. You will soon find that less of it will come your way.

Time Waster #7: Video Games

This includes phone games like Flappy Bird, home systems, tablet games, and every other form of electronic game available to you nowadays. While I can accept that kids enjoy them for entertainment and adults like them as a form of escapism, if the most used apps on your phone are games, you don't have a time problem; you have a priority problem.

THREE SIMPLE SOLUTIONS

1. Restrict game playing to certain predetermined flex times throughout the week. For instance, we simply don't allow our kids to play video games on their phones or elsewhere until after three p.m. during the summer. During the school year, video games can only be played on weekends.

2. Consider deleting all (or almost all) of the games from your phones or tablets and replacing them with smart, award-winning apps like Duolingo or Lumosity.

3. If you insist on playing, at least set hard limits on how long you will play, and consider playing only as a reward for certain milestones you hit. Think of 10,000 hours every time you open up one of those games.

HACKING YOUR SCHEDULE

I'm hesitant to advocate a strict way for you to manage your daily schedule, because each of us is radically different with unique demands being put on us. Studies have found that stay-at-home moms work the equivalent of two full-time jobs, but how they may need to manage their days is completely different from the schedule of someone who may have two clock-in/clock-out jobs outside of the home. Are you tracking with me? I want to advocate here, then, some unique ways you can hack your schedule to maximize your time no matter what your day looks like.

First, aim to eliminate enough of the time wasters from your daily life that you eventually have around two full hours per day to pursue your 100 life goals. This will seem less and less intimidating as we move forward and as you clarify your goals. Then establish at least two essential things you need to complete every day, and make sure the day doesn't end without your completing them. More than ever, pesky little e-mails and texts and phone calls and unplanned meetings can make it so that you finish an entire day without actually kicking the ball of your life very far down the field. With that in mind, try having two achievable accomplishments in mind by the time you finish breakfast in the morning, and aim to get those done as soon as possible at the start of your day.

Also, it's helpful to map out your schedule to the best of your ability. Some people I know map it out in very strict fifteen-minute blocks, and other people do it in two-to-three-hour blocks. Whatever type of flow works for you, map out what you need to get done and where you need to be ahead of time, so you can pace yourself accordingly. Otherwise, you will constantly feel like you are behind and the day is in charge of you versus the other way around.

Another great strategy is to use your phone to your advantage. Make use of the calendar feature on your phone, and sync it up with the calendar you use on your computer. I'm a Gmail guy, and Google does this really well. I also use my phone to take copious notes about thoughts and ideas I'm having throughout the day. I now use the Evernote app to better organize my thoughts and the photos and voice notes that I create. Another app I use is called Sleep Machine, to play background noise while I sleep, so that I'm not wasting time being bothered by other noises but am getting the most fulfilling rest during those hours. When I turn that app on, my mind

> **Telling my time what to do, instead of just going with the flow, means I get way more accomplished each day.**

and body know it's time to go to sleep. I also use the Fitbit app on my phone and pair it up with a bracelet I wear to track how active I am throughout the day. This motivates me to use every spare minute I have to hit my daily health goals. Begin seeing your phone as a device that can set you up for success versus draining your time and money!

Finally, use every spare moment smartly. I answer e-mails when I'm in line or waiting for a meeting to begin. I listen to audiobooks when I'm on the road or alone. I try to only use social media during my spare moments nowadays so that I can maximize my most focused time for other activities. I'm not robotic in my efforts, but I find that telling my time what to do, instead of just going with the flow, means I get way more accomplished each day.

KNOWING YOUR ENERGETIC RHYTHMS

Every person has a time of day when they feel, think, perform, and function the best. Elite athletes work hard to program their minds and bodies for that optimal time to be game time. You and I have our own "game time," and finding it and using it for the most important activities and work of our lives is essential. For a lot of the people I coach, their peak level of energy occurs two to two and a half hours after they wake up and get going for the day. For others, it may be at three p.m. or even later in the evening. Whatever your optimal time of day, it's important that you understand your energetic rhythms and do your most important work during your most energized time of day and your least important work during the low points of your day.

Regretfully, most people spend their best few hours answering random e-mails, texts, and phone calls—basically allowing other people to dictate the pace and activity of their day. When we give people permission to do business with us in this way, they will. We have to teach people the parameters of how we manage our daily schedule and ensure, whenever possible, that we work and com-municate with them on our best terms. If you are going to make significant progress on your life goals in the months and years ahead, getting a good groove with your daily schedule will be essential.

GETTING THINGS DONE

Hilariously, I was seriously considering making this chapter one sentence long. Here it is:

Buy the book *Getting Things Done: The Art of Stress-Free Productivity* by David Allen, and do at least half of what he suggests.

I'm not kidding. If all you did was take that advice, the quality of your life would go up, your stress level would go down, and you'd finally have more time to pursue your dreams and goals. No better, more practical book exists on time management and personal productivity. I'd love it if you read and instituted every principle and habit he shares, but even if you get only half of them integrated into your life, you will feel like a brand-new person. It's that good.

Don't worry; I don't have a referral deal with David Allen. I've never met him, but I'm a huge fan. When my life is operating on some of the basic principles from *Getting Things Done* (*GTD*), I feel limitless. When I abandon the things I've learned from *GTD*, I feel like I am in quicksand. On any given day I receive hundreds of non-spam e-mails and thousands of tweets and other social media interactions, have a dozen phone calls or video chats scheduled, and have urgent project deadlines pulling on every limb I have. Did I mention that my wife and I have kids in preschool, elementary school, middle school, and high school? Yeah. It gets crazy, and I'm not even talking about the honest demands of a good marriage, a sound spiritual life, and my constant call to be an outspoken leader. On any given day, with a few missteps, a flat tire, a sick child, or an unplanned conflict, my life can get overwhelming quickly if I allow it to do so. From the thousands of interviews I've done with people just like you, I've learned that your life, in spite of your well-intentioned to-do lists, often feels overwhelming, too. I want you to pick up *GTD*, from the library or bookstore, the first chance you get. It's going to make a real difference.

Joss Whedon, the revered director of Marvel's *The Avengers*, recently revealed that the principles he learned from *GTD* have changed his professional life. In an interview with *Fast Company*, Joss said, "You know, it's so easy to just get nothing done, but you've got to rock a little David Allen out to be able to get things done and break your list down into next actions. It has been enormously helpful, even in the baby steps version that I embrace."

So, I've made my strong pitch for *GTD*. I won't do it and you a disservice by trying to give you the summary version. Just know that what you learn there will help you get control of your life, better manage the overwhelming flow of information coming your way, and be more productive than you've probably ever been.

ONGOING MAINTENANCE

Even though they may have help, the best leaders in the world have the same twenty-four hours a day that you and I have. It doesn't matter if we're talking about the leaders of the free world, our favorite entertainers, or the best motivators and world changers on the planet. They each have the same amount of time to harness and use each day as you do. If anything, the most influential people in the world have more people pulling on them from every direction than any of us, and they must constantly labor to squeeze value out of every hour they have to work with.

As you move forward, you must understand that managing and maximizing your time is not a onetime occurrence but will require constant maintenance, oversight, and some occasional recalibration for you to stay on the right track. But please don't be intimidated. Once you get into a real groove with your time, you will find that you can accomplish more in a single day than you ever thought possible.

PART B

THINKING OF A MASTER PLAN

How Your Life Is About to Change

Thinking of a master plan

'Cause ain't nothing but sweat inside my hand.

—RAKIM, FROM THE SONG "PAID IN FULL"

A good plan today is better than a perfect plan tomorrow.

—GEORGE S. PATTON

Few people have any next, they live from hand to mouth without a

plan, and are always at the end of their line.

—RALPH WALDO EMERSON

Reduce your plan to writing. The moment you complete this, you will

have definitely given concrete form to the intangible desire.

—NAPOLEON HILL

Have you ever shown up to a long, mandatory meeting for your job . . . only to learn that not an ounce of planning or forethought went into it?

Have you ever pulled up at a restaurant drive-through, only for them to tell you that they were sold out of the very thing they're known for?

Have you ever shown up to a class or religious service and gotten the feeling that the speaker was completely unprepared and winging it?

I can kick it up a notch. . . .

Have you ever lived in a city experiencing severe weather and had to endure the fallout of how unprepared your government was for the disaster?

For the first thirteen years of my adult life I called Atlanta home. I graduated from Morehouse College in Atlanta, got my first real job as a schoolteacher in Atlanta, got married and had kids in Atlanta, started a church and a business in Atlanta. I love it there. However, every other winter it snows a few inches, and when it does the city shuts all the way down. I kid you not, if the weather forecasters predict snow in Atlanta, people raid the grocery stores like the zombie apocalypse is about to happen.

When I first saw people buying food and water like their lives depended on it because it was going to snow a few inches, I thought it was comical, ridiculous even. Entire grocery store shelves were empty. But the truth is when it snows an inch in Atlanta, it might as well snow ten feet, because the roads don't get salted properly and the state has very few trucks to clear the snow. What would have been a blip on the weather radar of cities like Chicago or New York completely crushes Atlanta.

Schools are shut down, hundreds of cars wreck on the black ice covering the roads, people are told to stay home from work, traffic jams highways so badly that people are forced to abandon their cars to try to walk home, and kids get stuck in schools and have to sleep there overnight with their teachers. It's insane! When it happened in 2003 we didn't have Twitter or Facebook to voice our complaints with, but when this same old story happened again in recent years, a full-fledged social media riot ensued and people demanded answers as to why the city and state were not better prepared since it happens every other winter.

We absolutely despise it when other people are not prepared, but the fact is that most of us are about as prepared for the road ahead as Georgia has ever been for a few inches of snow. As a general principle moving forward, it's only fair that you should be at least as prepared as you expect everybody else to be. The past four chapters were all about proactively addressing the roadblocks you are sure to face as you set and pursue your life goals. These next four chapters will help you change the trajectory of your life. We will talk about the key systems, strategies, and methodologies that you will use to craft your new life plan in a way that fuels real momentum and progress. Let's get started!

Happiness is not a matter of intensity but of balance, order,

rhythm and harmony.

—THOMAS MERTON

Next to love, balance is the most important thing.

—JOHN WOODEN

I believe that being successful means having a balance of

success stories across the many areas of your life. You can't

truly be considered successful in your business life if your home

life is in shambles.

—ZIG ZIGLAR

5

BALANCED ATTACK

The Seven Interlocking Life-Goal Categories

Balance is the four-leaf clover of all virtues. You'd know it if you saw it. You always hear about other lucky people finding it but never quite have it for yourself. In all my years of counseling and coaching, I have found that the pursuit of balance leaves more people frustrated than it does balanced. This is, in huge part, because people are pursuing an elusive myth of sorts. Balance is not perfection. It's not the permanent absence of conflict. Balance is not making life predictable.

I want to offer you a different way of thinking that is much less airy. At first it will feel just as impossible to execute as every other way, but I promise you it will get easier and easier as you continue to pursue it. The demands of work and life come in huge, often unpredictable waves, and the world will inevitably push and pull your mind, body, and soul in a million different directions. If anything, knowing this will help you anticipate the ebbs and flows of life at least a little bit more effectively, but it won't cause you to feel like a Zen guru if that's what you're expecting.

What, then, is true balance? True balance is having a plan for growth that you constantly pursue in each of the seven key areas of your life.

■ *Generosity:* How will I make the world a better place?

■ *Health and Fitness:* How will I give my body the best chance?

■ *Career and Finance:* How can I find financial freedom while doing what I love?

■ *Spirit and Emotion:* What will foster internal strength?

■ *Travel:* How can I grow by experiencing the beauty and people of the world?

■ *Friends and Family:* How can I make sure the people around me know how much I love them?

■ *Accomplishment and Experience:* What have I always dreamed of doing?

Later, we'll talk more about each of them and how to nail them down, but for now, I want you to take a mental leap with me.

CHANGING YOUR DEFAULT SETTINGS

You and I operate in life, day to day, month to month, year to year, with a complex array of default settings. The systems and habits that guide our decision-making are deeply embedded in who we are. For most of us, these were formed years and years ago and have changed very little over time. In fact, most of how you do in life was set before you ever moved out of the house and lived on your own. Some of us learned better habits and systems than others, but all of us, without fail, have a default way of doing things that could be seriously improved.

Very few of us come from a home in which all seven of the key areas above were regularly emphasized. I grew up in rural Kentucky with a single mother who worked in a brutally hot lightbulb factory for most of my childhood. We weren't even a little bit religious, we rarely traveled out of town, and my poor mother didn't often do anything for herself. Consequently, to this day, my default settings—the two values that probably guide my life the most—are the two that I learned from my mother: work like a dog and love family above all else. That's not a terrible starting point, but it lacks the balance needed to live a truly healthy life.

I'm going to be really transparent here. Don't judge me!

It's not in my default settings to care all that much about my physical or emotional health. It's not in my default settings to build wealth or make investments. It's not in my default settings to care about religious or spiritual matters. If I have a good family unit and a job that pays the bills, I am pretty hardwired not to care much about anything else. Now, if you know me as the guy who created charities that gave away millions of dollars, or as the man who started a church in inner-city Atlanta, or as the dad of a globe-trotting, homeschooling family, then it might be a real surprise to you that those things don't come easy for me.

In fact, like most people, when I am stressed out or in a bind for some reason, I am prone to dropping everything around me that isn't a part of my default settings. I'll throw myself into my work and stop thinking about anything or anybody that isn't work or family related. It's not healthy, but it's normal.

The problem is that normal is not good enough to bust you out of mediocrity. Normal doesn't have the power to take you from where you are to where you dream of being.

For you, your default settings may be to be very religious and shockingly generous, and you may feel most at peace when you are in one of those two zones. I have a very close family member who has those default settings. At face value, you could do much worse than being a very generous person who loves God, but the limitations of those default settings have caused her to struggle mightily in every other area of her life.

> **Normal is not good enough to bust you out of mediocrity.**

Building your life on any narrow default settings is generally a bad idea. Depending on what defaults you have, you may not crash and burn for the whole world to see, as some celebrities do, but you may still live a life far below your potential. One could argue that it is equally tragic to do so quietly as it is to do so publicly.

When we abandon our physical health, for example, and put all of our eggs in a religious basket, we aren't able to truly live out the tenets of our faith, which require us to be active and mobile. When we ignore our financial health but work out three times a day, we have the benefits of being fit but all the struggles of being broke—which makes being fit much less cool. You get where I'm going with this?

While we like to live as if each unique area of our life is an island unto itself, it just doesn't work that way and never will. Problems in one area pretty much touch all seven areas of your life in detrimental ways.

Completely ignoring huge swaths of your life prevents you from fully enjoying and maximizing the benefits of what you actually do well. Even if your primary goal isn't to be a more balanced person but to enjoy your strengths more, it's in your best interest to have a balanced approach to your entire life.

See, most of us have a weird way—and I understand why—of thinking that our default settings are somehow superior to those held by other people. Because work and family are my main thing, when I see people who are wired differently, I'm prone to judging them in my mind. I've come to learn that people who are hardwired to be physically fit or financially savvy often make the same mistake and wonder why other people can't step up and lose weight or get out of debt. You and I know, though, that it's very hard to excel outside of your default settings.

But if you are going to have substantial, sustainable change in your life, it's going to require you to change those default settings. You are going to have to transition away from doing what's comfortable and into a new way of living that gives a balanced amount of time, energy, and resources to all seven of the key areas of your life.

But how do you do that?

1. Think Back to Your Childhood

I'm not here to psychoanalyze you. I also don't want to spend too much extra time talking about fringe theories that you may or may not believe. I do, though, need you to accept the basic reality that much of who you are and why you are the way you are comes from the lessons and experiences, both good and bad, that you had during your formative childhood years. A lot of what you and I learned we don't even remember learning—it's just a part of us now. Some of the lessons weren't taught as much as observed. In fact, most of what we learned as children about the seven interlocking life-goal categories didn't come as a result of a teacher in front of a chalkboard; it came from watching our parents, guardians, siblings, and even friends.

In my workshops on diversity, I often explain to people that they are what they are way more than they even have the capacity to understand. If you grew up in the high-rise projects of Queens, New York, in the 1980s with a drug-dealing single mother, it's going to leave an indelible mark on how you view yourself and the world. That's the rapper 50 Cent.

If you grew up on a tobacco farm in rural Kentucky with overtly racist parents and very little interaction with people other than your immediate family, it's going to influence your worldview in very deep ways. I grew up with a lot of young boys and girls who were raised just that way, and they hated my friends and me without ever really getting to know us. That's how racism works.

I see it like this: all of us are whiter, blacker, browner, richer, poorer, more liberal, more conservative, more Southern, more Northern, more Western, more Eastern, than we ever fully understand. You don't wake up in the morning and think of yourself as a wealthy, liberal Latino from Southern California. You just wake up and go, like everybody else does. However, beneath the surface of our daily lives exists our default ways of seeing the world, and yours came greatly from childhood.

I'd like for you to take a look again at the seven categories, but don't think about how you view them now. I want you to think about how your parents, grandparents, and immediate family viewed them when you were a child. Did they completely ignore any of the categories? Were they particularly great at any of them? How did they assign value, or lack thereof, to each one?

Generosity
Health and Fitness
Career and Finance
Spirit and Emotion
Travel
Friends and Family
Accomplishment and Experience

Now I'd like for you to consider what you learned about each of the seven life-goal categories as a child. What did you observe?

What were you expressly taught? How did it impact who you are and aren't today? Feel free to think these things through or write them down in a journal or file that you can refer back to later if needed.

Don't get me wrong; you aren't defined by your childhood. Like many of yours did, my childhood had a lot of painful moments. I just want us to acknowledge that all of those moments, good and bad, play a significant role in how we see the world today. Our job will be to clarify how they have defined us and move forward from there.

2. Identify Your Defaults

Now let's do the hard work of identifying the top two default areas of your life. It's important for us to do this, because we will use them later when we form your unique life goals. It will also help you understand recurring patterns in your life.

Which two of the seven areas come most naturally to you? Yes, you must pick two and only two.

As I said earlier, for me, my family and my career are obvious default strengths for me. Notice that I didn't say "Friends and Family" or "Career and Finance." Within those two categories, my default is pretty narrow and only includes my family and my career. I've never been great with friends or finance, and it requires a lot of extra effort for me to thoughtfully tend to each of them.

My wife, on the other hand, is spiritual and generous with ease. Because we've been together since we were young teenagers, I've watched her grow in other areas, such as her career as a teacher and her development as an expert traveler all around the world, but at her core more than these other roles is a deeply giving, spiritual woman. Because of this, Rai and I approach crises in drastically different ways. Neither is completely right or wrong—they're just different.

What are your two? I want to caution you not to pick the two you wish you had but the two you actually have. It's very likely that one or both of them are directly connected to your childhood—either because you observed them in the people you loved or because you rebelled against traits that affected you. For instance, many of my closest friends who had deeply religious parents working full-time in religious professions are now some of the least religious people I know. They saw too much of the pain in the profession and chose to go in the opposite direction.

Whatever the case is with you, identifying your two default areas is an essential step in moving forward.

3. Identify Your Weaknesses

As important as it is to understand your strengths, it's even more important that you consider your weaknesses. It's these weaknesses that will pull you down, slow your progress, and keep you from having true momentum in life as you pursue your dreams and goals. If ignored, your weaknesses will not only become stumbling blocks, but they will greatly lessen the potential impact of your strengths. Eliminate your two strengths from the list. Which of the remaining five areas are difficult for you? Don't be embarrassed; you may have a few areas that are completely nonexistent in your life. This is obviously a good sign that they are weaknesses for you.

For some people, identifying these areas of weakness helps them to better understand fears and past failures. Why do you have these weaknesses? How have they negatively impacted you throughout your life? How would your life improve if these areas were actually strengths?

While I honestly believe that you are fully capable of becoming a master in the areas of your weaknesses, our initial goals are just going to be for you to become aware of them and then to grow to a point of competence with them. For instance, if you could become reasonably fit physically, it would have an amazingly positive, uplifting effect on several things just as much as having terrible health negatively affects every other area of your life.

What are your two weakest areas?

4. Identify the Middle

Now that you've picked your two strengths and two weaknesses, the three in the middle should be easy to identify. These are likely skills that you developed in adulthood. You may actually be great at these things now, but they aren't necessarily your default strengths. For instance, my wife and I had very similar childhoods where we moved a lot from home to home, but within a small geographical area. Our parents rarely traveled outside of the American South their entire lives. Rai and I, though, had something built into us that was comfortable with moving since we had moved so often (over thirty-five times between the two of us), so we took traveling to another level. We have visited more than half the states in the US, lived all over the country, and started traveling the world with our big family on a shoestring budget. It's definitely not our weakness.

When he was first drafted by the Chicago Bulls, Michael Jordan, now thought of as the best basketball player ever, became an offensive powerhouse right out of the gate. Within a few years he was leading the league in scoring, and the Bulls regularly made it to the play-offs. However, for some reason, MJ couldn't take his team to the next level. At that point he started focusing a lot of his on-court energy and off-court practice on becoming a defensive stopper. What was once a liability for Jordan soon became a major strength. In 1988 Jordan was named the NBA Defensive Player of the Year—an award rarely given to a player of his offensive caliber. From that point on, he was regularly one of the top defensive players in the league. Scoring was always his key strength, but he learned to make his man-on-man defense a secondary strength that changed the entire trajectory of his career.

That's what we want your middle strengths to be. They may not be your natural gifts, but they can be learned skills that make your top strengths better and your core weaknesses less of a liability.

5. Pledge to Make the Change

The first step to change is always making your mind up that you are going to do it. It's also not a onetime decision but a decision you have to reaffirm over and over again. Living life purely

> **The first step to change is always making your mind up that you are going to do it.**

off your one or two natural gifts and strengths is not sustainable and will cause you to hit walls unnecessarily as you break out of your comfort zone to pursue your life goals. Forgive me if this sounds cheesy, but I want you to read and repeat the following affirmations several times. Get them deep inside of you. As we move forward together your mind is going to have to be completely made up.

I will not allow my weaknesses to remain the way they are.
I will put my life on the path to growth.
My dreams deserve the best chance I can give them.
I will take direct steps toward living a balanced life.

Now read and repeat these affirmations a few more times before moving on.

MOVING FORWARD

I'm very proud of you for taking these early steps. Soon you will see the benefits. Together, the seven interlocking life-goal categories are going to lift your entire life up from the ground level. A huge part of the magic that will happen here requires incremental growth in all seven areas versus a hyper-focus on just one or two.

As we move forward, you must resist the urge to focus only on what you know and do well, for it will be the new growth in your old areas of weakness that will unlock doors and portals into the future you never imagined possible. It may be hard for you to see yourself excelling in these fresh, new ways, but I assure you that your mind will be increasingly open to what's possible as you experience the thrill of progress in your life.

Buckle up! Your entire life is about to change.

It must be borne in mind that the tragedy of life doesn't lie in not reaching your goal. The tragedy lies in having no goal to reach. It isn't a calamity to die with dreams unfulfilled, but it is a calamity not to dream. It is not a disaster to be unable to capture your ideal, but it is a disaster to have no ideal to capture. It is not a disgrace not to reach the stars, but it is a disgrace to have no stars to reach for. Not failure, but low aim is sin.

—DR. BENJAMIN ELIJAH MAYS

Twenty years from now you will be more disappointed by the things that you didn't do than by the ones you did do. So throw off the bowlines. Sail away from the safe harbor. Catch the trade winds in your sails. Explore. Dream. Discover.

—H. JACKSON BROWN JR.

If you have built castles in the air, your work need not be lost; that is where they should be. Now put the foundations under them.

—HENRY DAVID THOREAU

YORGs (YOUR OUTRAGEOUSLY RIDICULOUS GOALS)

Seven Goals That Guide Them All

'll be the first one to admit that life has a sad way of squeezing the loftiness out of our dreams and goals. We went from wanting to be astronauts, athletes, and award-winning entertainers to getting happy when we pay our credit card bill before a late fee hits. The correlation between aging and the decline of ambition is staggering. When a good night's rest is no longer the thing that fuels our dreams but the dream itself, something's wrong. In fact, most adults have either stopped dreaming about the future altogether or shifted from dreaming for themselves to dreaming for their kids or someone/something else, like a sports team or celebrity.

Listen. I get it. Life can be hard. Real hard! Bills, career shifts, disappointments, deaths, health challenges, relationship problems, increasing responsibilities, and sheer exhaustion can make dreaming about your own future seem like a big waste of time, but I assure you, it isn't. Whether you need to blow all the dust and cobwebs off your old dreams or open up your mind to brand-new ones, having them and embracing them with your whole heart is an essential step. It may not be easy for you, but you can push past all the excuses you tell yourself about why you are destined for mediocrity or why you should just stop reading this book now and go watch a game show. Don't believe the lie that you are too old to dream big!

Stan Lee, the creator of Spider-Man, the Hulk, Iron Man, the X-Men, and so many other iconic superheroes, was thirty-nine years old before he created any of those characters!

Julia Child, one of the most famous chefs of the twentieth century, didn't even learn to cook until she was thirty-three and first appeared on television when she was fifty years old!

A struggling milk shake machine salesman, Ray Kroc was fifty-two years old when he poured everything he had into building McDonald's into a global burger franchise.

Laura Ingalls Wilder was sixty-five years old when she published her first novel based on her childhood in rural Kansas, entitled *Little House in the Big Woods*, and followed it up with *Farmer Boy* and *Little House on the Prairie* several years later.

Nola Ochs was a whopping ninety-five years old when she earned her bachelor's degree, and she shocked the world when she earned her master's degree three years later!

If they weren't too old to do what they did, you aren't too old to go hard after your dreams either!

Before we can dive into building a comprehensive life plan that actually works, though, we need to set a solid foundation for that plan. I like to say that a bucket list is better than nothing, but not by much. Without a foundation, a starting point, a strategic plan, and some real momentum, bucket lists usually end up forgotten, lost, or worse—they can even have the unintended consequence of making the author feel like a failure for being unable to achieve anything on the list.

Like all solid foundations, this one cannot be built overnight. It's going to take some real time, energy, and craftsmanship. It's going to require you to dig deep and dream again. It's going to force you to take the beautiful but often abstract dreams of your heart and soul and morph them into actionable goals. Sometimes we prefer to keep dreams inside of us, because they can look and feel so magical when they don't require words or budgets or deadlines or scrutiny of any kind. I get it. I just need you to understand that you are doing your best dreams the worst disservice by keeping them a secret. By selling them short, you are selling yourself and anybody who has ever poured an ounce of effort into you short.

The concrete, the bricks, the building blocks that we are about to use are called YORGs—Your Outrageously Ridiculous Goals. You will be creating just one powerhouse YORG for each of the seven interlocking life-goal categories. Even more than it is in most of this book, it's particularly important that you *do not* skip ahead or rush through this chapter. The YORGs you craft are going to color and add flavor to every other goal you create. While I love rapid progress as much as the next man, this is one of those times where I'm going to ask you to slow your pace so that you give the creation of each and every YORG your best shot. It's that important.

SAMPLE YORGs—*GENEROSITY*

▪ Start and lead a creative and performing arts high school in inner-city Atlanta by August 1, 2020. Funded by private/public partnerships, the school should have a minimum rating of 9 on GreatSchools and have over 90 percent of students either go straight to college or be placed in a related career.

▪ By January 1, 2040, I want my direct work, fund-raising, and advocacy to be responsible for freeing/rescuing over 100,000 people from human trafficking/modern-day slavery.

BREAKING DOWN *YORG*

Your

Each of the YORGs you create to lead the seven life-goal categories must be completely and uniquely your own. That doesn't mean that you can't be inspired by other people, but a YORG has to belong to you. It needs to have an anchor in your heart. You have to want it . . . badly. All seven YORGs may not be ideas or dreams you've had for years and years, but at least a few of them need to have some history in your mind. Even if they are new, never-before-expressed ideas, they must come from your essence and be a clear expression of your best self. It's fine if your YORGs are somehow informed by what you've witnessed someone else accomplish from afar, but your rationale for making them the most important goals of your life must be personal.

When life gets hard—and it will—it's going to be very important that you have a vision for the future firmly and deeply rooted in your own reality and not in mine or anyone else's. It's highly unlikely that my YORGs are going to look anything like yours. My crazy life is totally different from yours. Because of this, understand now that your YORGs will always make more sense to you than they do to anybody else, and when you find somebody who actually gets and digs your YORGs, call them friend and keep them forever!

SAMPLE YORGs—*HEALTH AND FITNESS*

▪ Complete at least five Ironman triathlons before my forty-fifth birthday on September 16, 2025, and place in the top twenty-five of at least two of them.

▪ Successfully climb to the top of the highest mountain on each of the seven continents (known as the Seven Summits) by January 30, 2022. Take a family member with me to the top for at least three of the climbs.

Outrageously

When you look at your life today, then look at the seven YORGs you create, something should be missing. If you see a straight, predictable path to the YORG, it's not big enough. Each YORG should stretch your limits and cause you to grow, so much so that the right-now version of you simply doesn't have what it takes to complete it. The level of guts, audacity, tenacity, courage, strength, and vision required, coupled with the resources you will need to complete each YORG, should be radically different from where you are at this moment. If being normal gets you what you've always gotten, it's time for you to be outrageous.

SAMPLE YORGs—*CAREER AND FINANCE*

▉ Become a tenured professor of history at an Ivy League university by August 1, 2030.

▉ Become a majority owner of a professional sports team in the NBA, the NFL, or MLB by July 16, 2035.

Ridiculous

I deliberately included what looks like the same word twice in this acronym. *Outrageously*, though, describes how it looks to you. *Ridiculous* is how your goals are going to look to everybody else! It's possible people may laugh out loud when they learn about these YORGs. After all, *ridiculous* shares the same root word as *ridicule*. In fact, when other people hear that you have these goals, it should shock them and maybe even make them a little uncomfortable, either because they can't believe they think so small or they can't wrap their minds around what gives you the nerve to think so big. More than anything, though, a YORG cannot be something that people achieve every day. It has to be so difficult to accomplish that people feel like you are crazy for even considering it.

At the same time, please do not worry. With time, effort, and the right resources, you can and will make what used to look ridiculous to everybody else a reality in your own life.

Goal

Goals are very different from dreams or ideas. Goals are dreams with deadlines and budgets. Goals have action steps. Goals are measurable. They exist in time and space. Goals require forward progress and momentum. Sadly, most of our hopes and dreams never quite make it to the goal stage. Goals have a beginning, middle, and end. Goals have an expected finish line. Goals are clearly articulated and understood. You can train and prepare to reach a goal.

SAMPLE YORGs—*SPIRIT AND EMOTION*

▪ Visit the fifty most spiritual sites in the world as described by *National Geographic* before December 25, 2040.

▪ Privately ask for forgiveness from every person I've ever wronged, and grant forgiveness to every person who ever wronged me. Follow up by leading an online class on forgiveness with over 100 attendees by January 1, 2021.

WHAT YORGs ARE

Despite how it may seem, YORGs are not simply a random list of ideas, but the backbone of your entire strategic life plan. The many additional goals you develop in the seven life-goal categories will contribute toward building the skills, confidence, relationships, and resources you need to eventually achieve those overarching goals that would seem close to impossible today. Carefully crafting your seven YORGs will set the tone for every other goal you develop and pursue.

While each of your individual goals must be well articulated, this will be doubly true for the seven YORGs you craft. In addition to really taking some time to think, study, research, and even pray about each YORG, you will need to take about an hour or so to write and edit each one to make sure it can stand the test of time. An early mistake people frequently make is to not be specific enough. Make sure all your goals moving forward are detailed and unmistakably specific. Each YORG needs to have a month, day, and year you will achieve it by. Part of giving each YORG a due date is to make it real for you and to give yourself some healthy pressure to actually position your life to accomplish it. When we avoid deadlines for our dreams, we delay them indefinitely.

SAMPLE YORGs—*TRAVEL*

▨ Visit and camp out with my family at every national park in the United States by May 6, 2032.

▨ Visit TripAdvisor's top twenty-five beaches of the world, and take a selfie with my wife with our feet in the water at each one by September 5, 2035.

By having extremely ambitious YORGs, you will be compelled to move forward with all the other goals in each category. For instance, if your YORG in the Health and Fitness category is to successfully climb to the top of the highest mountain in each of the seven continents by January 30, 2022, achieving such a lofty goal is going to assume that you hit other preliminary goals in the Health and Fitness category, but also in the Career and Finance category, Travel, and more. In other words, your YORGs need to be so ambitious that they require you to put in real work in almost every area of your life.

Each YORG you create needs to be a culmination of sorts. While the other goals may be stepping-stones, a YORG is a milestone moment. For instance, for a Generosity YORG someone may say they want to sign the Warren Buffett/Bill Gates pledge by March 18, 2037, for billionaires to give away half of their wealth in their lifetime. In other words, you are not only going to need to be a billionaire to sign the pledge (which is going to assume a lot of other things about your life), but you are also pledging to have causes you want to give at least $500 million to. When I say that YORGs are culminating events, it doesn't mean you are done in that area of your life when you achieve the YORG, but it will mean it's a pivotal point for you, a time when you will begin to consider new adventures and challenges to pursue.

WHAT YORGs AREN'T

Even though the very definition of a YORG is that it is outrageously ridiculous, it shouldn't be something that is impossible. If you are forty-two years old and haven't played football since middle school, having a YORG of becoming the MVP of the NFL as a quarterback for a Super Bowl championship team isn't just outrageously ridiculous; it's also impossible and dumb. While each YORG you create should push the boundaries of impossibility, it should stop just short of crossing the line itself. For instance, if you want to have a *New York Times* bestselling book that Oprah Winfrey reads and loves, then that goal, while audacious, isn't impossible.

Friends, family, coaches, advisers, guides, financiers, and more may all be needed to help you make a YORG possible, but the bulk of the work has to be done by you and the result of the YORG cannot be up to other people. For instance, YORGs that require you to be something like the "most loved attorney in New York City" or the "most famous singer in California" not only make it too difficult to measure your success but put the primary burden of the goal on people other than yourself. Instead of trying to be the most famous singer in California, you could base your goal on album sales or concert attendance or a particular award you want to win.

SAMPLE YORGs—*FRIENDS AND FAMILY*

■ Surprise ten married couples among my friends and family with ten different all-expenses-paid vacations on their wedding anniversaries by September 22, 2030.

■ Write and publish a *New York Times* bestselling book on marriage with my wife by Valentine's Day of 2020.

Another pitfall to watch out for is how cheap and quickly achievable the YORG you're considering is. If you have the time, money, and skills today to achieve a goal, then it's absolutely not a YORG. YORGs are costly, and I don't just mean financially. They will cost you years of preparation, hard work, networking, growth, and experience. If you can achieve it in the next year or two, it's not big enough. As I am writing this book, I am seriously considering applying for a particular PhD program. It's a long shot that I would even be accepted, but if I was, it would take me at least five years to complete the program. So, even though that means I could have a PhD in five years, the goal is not outrageously ridiculous enough. A more ambitious goal that would still require me to have a PhD would be to become a tenured professor at an Ivy League university or a college president. Those two goals, which would require a PhD, would also require much more than just a PhD.

In other words, whatever your goal is, think three to four steps beyond that goal in terms of the optimal success you could have if you achieved the initial goal, and make one of the steps way down the line into your YORG for that category.

TIME TO CRAFT YOUR YORGS

Okay! This is where the rubber meets the road. It's time for you to craft one YORG for each of the seven life-goal categories. Even if your typical way of doing things is to barrel through tasks like a bull in a china shop, I'm asking you to slow down on this one. It needs to be right.

Don't jump ahead and start writing all 100 of your life goals yet. Now is a good time, though, to begin brainstorming about all of the dreams, thoughts, and ideas you've had over the years in each category. Some are going to flow and come out very easily, and others are going to be really tough to craft. It's perfectly normal for you to write and rewrite your YORGs several times before settling on some amazing goals that you can be proud of. While you should plan to give yourself a few days (but no more than a week) to craft the first draft of your YORGs, just know that you are going to have plenty of time to edit and refine them in the future.

SAMPLE YORGs—*ACCOMPLISHMENT AND EXPERIENCE*

■ **Earn a true black belt in Brazilian jiujitsu and win first place in my division in a national tournament by January 1, 2035.**

■ **Teach an advanced grilling course at one of the most prestigious culinary schools in the country by July 4, 2024.**

Below is a reminder of the seven questions to get your mind moving in each category. Think over the questions, open your mind, dream again, then start typing or handwriting your responses in a safe place. Good luck!

■ *Generosity:* How will I make the world a better place?

■ *Health and Fitness:* How will I give my body the best chance?

- *Career and Finance:* How can I find financial freedom while doing what I love?

- *Spirit and Emotion:* What will foster internal strength?

- *Travel:* How can I grow by experiencing the beauty and people of the world?

- *Friends and Family:* How can I make sure the people around me know how much I love them?

- *Accomplishment and Experience:* What have I always dreamed of doing?

Success comes from taking the initiative and following up . . .
persisting . . . eloquently expressing the depth of your love.
What simple action could you take today to produce a new
momentum toward success in your life?

—TONY ROBBINS

Whatever beginning goals you set for yourself, following through
on them will build momentum and a sense of achievement and
those small successes will point the way to bigger ones.

—PAMELA GLASS KELLY

If you don't design your own life plan, chances are you'll fall into
someone else's plan. And guess what they have planned for
you? Not much.

—JIM ROHN

7

THE LIFE-GOAL FIREBALL

Getting Momentum and Keeping It

At the core of my being, I'm a starter. I've started charities, churches, and businesses all over the world. Starters are a unique breed of people. We love the thrill of taking a small seed of an idea and doing the difficult but exciting work of growing what was once but a passing thought into a real product or company. Starting may be where the excitement is, but with each year that has passed in my life, I've grown to understand that while starting a project may be exhilarating, building it into something that thrives, lasts, and stands the test of time is what really proves your maturity. Time and time again, I see new entrepreneurs make the mistake that I used to make in thinking that the brilliance of a really phenomenal idea plays a bigger role in the success of that idea than it really does.

The truth is that if you see or use a product in the marketplace today, whether it is an online platform or a tangible item that you love to purchase, it's very likely that it beat out many other more spectacular ideas that just didn't have the same management or momentum. Nothing's better than a brilliant idea that's brilliantly executed, but a good idea that's brilliantly executed will trump a brilliant idea that's poorly executed ten times out of ten. While starting something great indeed takes courage and tenacity, it's when we are able to maintain something great that real life change begins to happen.

I want you to hear from a self-proclaimed starter that the importance of my greatest gift is, if not overrated, at least exaggerated at the expense of the essential

> **A good idea that's brilliantly executed will trump a brilliant idea that's poorly executed ten times out of ten.**

steps that come after you start down a great and noble path. Many a New Year's resolution gets off to a rousing start for a few hours—sometimes even a few days—but, without fail, it struggles to keep any semblance of the momentum with which it was started. The same is true for weight-loss plans or new ways to budget your money or keep your house clean. We want to see and experience the change that comes with new habits, but old habits do die hard.

The one thing that I *have* seen consistently steamroll over old habits is positive, forward-moving momentum. It rarely happens by accident, and if you ever do get some without great, deliberate effort, I assure you that you can only keep momentum on purpose. In an instant-gratification culture, well-meaning adults give up on quality self-help programs in hours or days, because their minds are programmed to see real change happen before it's physically possible. You can have six-pack abs; you just can't have them tomorrow or even next week. But you could have them in six to twelve months. Since you aim to be around in six to twelve months anyway, you might as well do what you need to do to have six-pack abs, but most people give up before they build the necessary momentum to see results.

To help you get momentum and keep it, I've developed something called the life-goal fireball. The principles behind it will shape everything about how you set, list, and pursue your 100 life goals. Stick with me for a few minutes, and we'll soon begin building out your 100 life goals together.

THE FIRE TRIANGLE

Time and time again, people get frustrated and discouraged when they set out to make substantive life changes and don't see measurable results right away. They fail to realize that life change is complicated, like wildfire, and not only requires the right ingredients to get started, but a very particular set of conditions to grow and develop.

Seasoned firefighters know that three primary factors are required for a fire to start, stay lit, and eventually spread. These three factors are called the fire triangle and include fuel to burn, air to supply oxygen, and a heat source to spark the fire. Firefighters have found that if they can eliminate any one of these three items, they can control and eventually extinguish the fire. But there are also two variables that can cause small fires to grow into big ones: the weather and the terrain. So, as you can imagine, when the fire triangle is in place, coupled with dry, windy weather and the perfect terrain of wood and brush, it creates nearly unstoppable conditions for a fire to grow.

Fuel to Burn

In forest fires, the fuel to burn is ample and ranges from pinecones, needles, and dry brush to all sizes of trees, large and small. For you, your 100 life goals are the fuel to burn. Like in the forest, we are deliberately making it so that you have a wide variety of goals, ranging from small ones that catch fire easily (brush and pinecones), to goals you could achieve in a few months to a year but will build momentum as you achieve them (small trees), all the way to enormous goals and YORGs, which will undoubtedly require many years to accomplish (large trees).

Air to Supply Oxygen

Without wind from the outside, forest fires wouldn't spread. In your life, you are bound to have moments when you have all the ingredients for your life goals to really catch on, but you just don't have the wind from the outside required to gain momentum. I want to suggest three types of outside wind sources that can keep the fire of your life goals growing. The first is coaching like you are receiving now from me, but also from other leaders and experts who've already been where you are trying to go. I completely neglected this aspect of my life until the past few years and have since found that good coaching has helped me grow exponentially faster than

I ever could have on my own. Second, the camaraderie of peers is something that could really help you on this journey. We have our own 100 Life Goals communities that you can join, or you can form your own community, large or small, to keep you focused, encouraged, and growing. Last—and this is more specialized for those of you who see yourselves as spiritual or even religious—prayer and meditation are powerful tools with benefits that I couldn't begin to overstate.

A Heat Source to Spark the Fire

Amazingly, the largest forest fires often start with just the spark of a single match. Like that match, your decision to start on the journey toward setting and pursuing 100 life goals is going to be all the spark you need to set the fuel on fire. Like most deserving endeavors, though, you won't decide just once to pursue it; you are going to have to decide over and over again that you are sticking with your decision. Sometimes the fire will get low, and it will need you to stoke it and keep it lit. You may do this by rereading your 100 life goals or by checking in online to see how other people are doing in their pursuits. As silly as it may sound, when I need a little motivation I love to watch the movie *Rocky IV*. For you, I am sure it will be something different, but it's important to have a song or a movie or a book that gives you a little extra spark when you need it the most.

UPHILL MOMENTUM

When I studied how forest fires start and grow and spread, perhaps the most amazing thing I learned was that forest fires behave in a way that's surprising and quite counterintuitive. A forest fire moves faster up hills and steep slopes than it does downhill. This is in large part because winds tend to move uphill and carry the flames up slopes and even over enormous mountains. Because of this, forest fires grow rapidly in mountainous terrain with steep slopes and slowly on flat plains. We are going to use this same principle of uphill momentum as we craft your 100 life goals.

Now, let's get to work.

Go to 100LifeGoals.com for the worksheet we are about to use. It's entitled "Life-Goal Fireball." You can also create one yourself on a Google spreadsheet or Excel document, or even a blank sheet of paper if you want to go real old-school with it. My preference is that you use an electronic method that you can save and update easily, but it's not required if you don't have access to technology.

Here, again, are the seven life-goal categories:

1. Generosity

2. Health and Fitness

3. Career and Finance

4. Spirit and Emotion

5. Travel

6. Friends and Family

7. Accomplishment and Experience

In addition to a YORG, each category will help you work toward creating a dozen or so goals. You will naturally find some categories much easier than others. The ones that come easily for you may end up with fifteen (maybe even more), and the ones that don't may only have ten goals. If, at the end of your first run at this, you've made fewer than 100 life goals, don't worry. Trust me; you will soon be adding new goals to the empty slots very quickly.

The Building Goals

Each category needs to have two goals you can complete in the next two months. These goals are the pinecones and needles and brush that we need to light right away to get your fire going. I cannot stress enough how important it is that you get these early victories under your belt. These first baby steps are absolutely indispensable. If you've ever tried to build a campfire without brush, you've discovered just how hard it is to light a log with a match. It really doesn't work. However, that's basically what we try to do when we pursue huge life goals without anything to give us momentum, to get us rolling beforehand.

These early goals must be as close to free as they possibly can be. If you happen to have money to spare for them, that's fine, but I don't want lack of money to be an early excuse for you to stop pursuing these goals. If you have, for instance, a Generosity YORG to free 100,000 people from human trafficking, I would suggest two initial goals in that category to be something like reading the best-reviewed books on human trafficking, beginning training to become a volunteer for organizations in your area, applying for an internship or job at a top organization in the field, beginning a monthly donation to organizations fighting trafficking, finding and registering for the best conferences on the topic, and signing up for every newsletter and following every anti–human trafficking leader on social media.

You get where I'm going with this? The first two goals in each category need to help you add knowledge, skills, expertise, legitimacy, and relationships that will move you forward toward much larger goals down the road. Don't simply see these goals as stepping-stones to the "real ones." These are as real as any others and are equally important. Don't blow through them carelessly, but act as if the quality of the new way you're going to do life depends on them.

Next you will need to set three goals in each category that you can complete in one year or less. At least one of these goals should be directly tied to your YORG, and the other two can be electives of sorts. Those elective goals obviously need to fit in the category but don't have to necessarily be directly related to your YORG. If you can set goals that are even loosely connected, then great, but it's not required. These goals should increase in difficulty and com-mitment from your initial two goals. Some may require you to save money for a few months or to take a few days off of work for travel. If your budget is very tight, you can still have goals in this category that are low-cost financially but will require a heavy investment of time. Writing a book or performing a nine-month internship comes to mind. You must never allow excuses to derail you in these crucial early stages.

Each goal you create needs to be progressively more difficult than the one before it, and as much as possible, you need to pursue them in order, like this:

- Goal 1: Easiest goal on list—completed in less than two months

- Goal 2: Slightly harder than goal 1—completed in less than two months

- Goal 3: Slightly harder than goal 2—completed in less than one year and directly tied to your YORG

- Goal 4: Slightly harder than goal 3, but clearly harder than goals 1 and 2—completed in less than one year (elective goal)

- Goal 5: Slightly harder than goal 4, but clearly harder than goals 1–3—completed in less than one year (elective goal)

When life presents you with an amazing opportunity to achieve a goal out of order, carefully consider how legitimate the opportunity is, and go for it if it feels right in your gut. If not, give it a wink, and keep it moving. It's probably just a distraction, and you'll have plenty of those.

The Growing Goals

If goals one through five were bushes, shrubs, and small trees for the fire, goals six through ten are the large trees of the forest. Because of the experience you will have gained by achieving the building goals, these huge goals will no longer look or feel nearly as impossible or intimidating as they would have had you skipped the early steps (like most people try to do) and gone right to these.

In fact, whenever I hear of somebody being an overnight sensation, I laugh to myself, because most overnight sensations were working diligently on things like the building goals before they blew up. They are only overnight sensations to the people who didn't know they were working their butts off long before they became famous. That's our aim for you, too. If luck is preparation meeting opportunity, goals one through five are that preparation for the opportunities that will start coming.

Goals six through ten are serious commitments. They are audacious, occasionally expensive, and will require an enormous amount of effort and energy to accomplish. This is you getting your law degree and your MBA. This is you losing every pound that you need to lose and running three full marathons. This is you paying off 100 percent of your debt. This is you moving across the world and buying a home in another country. This is you summiting Mount Everest. This is you writing your four-book series for kids. This is you getting hired and promoted, twice, at your dream job. This is you starting the third location of the restaurant franchise you've dreamed of. This is you testing as fluent in a foreign language. This is you traveling on a human-trafficking rescue mission and succeeding. This is you having 10,000,000 downloads of your second app.

In five years or less, if you are determined to be your completely focused best self, you can pretty much accomplish 95 percent of your life goals. Some of them will throw you for a loop and take longer, and some will shock you and be easier than you planned. The key, though, is that you will be on track to achieving your YORG and living the life that you've always imagined. We have hundreds of thousands of hours to live, and if we live them well, we can see and experience the world and leave it better than we found it.

The Stretch Goals

Finally, right underneath your YORG in each category are two goals that will take you longer than five years to achieve. These goals are almost as audacious and difficult as your YORGs and will absolutely take your achieving all ten earlier goals to make them happen. These stretch goals would be things like becoming the general manager of the Los Angeles Lakers, becoming CEO of American Express, winning a Nobel Prize, or winning an Academy Award for best documentary. Think big; think outrageous. Imagine what you could do right now if you had all the skills, relationships, and resources you will gain from achieving goals one through ten. *Then* imagine what's possible. These goals are ridiculous now, but they won't seem that way in ten years.

In summary:

1. One YORG in each category

2. Two goals in each category you can complete in two months (should be close to free and at least loosely related to your YORG)

3. Three goals in each category you can complete in one year (should increase in commitment and cost, and some should be related to your YORG)

4. Five goals in each category that will take one to five years each (should increase in commitment and cost, and some should be related to your YORG)

5. Two goals in each category that will absolutely take more than five years to achieve (one should be related to your YORG)

THE WEATHER OF OUR LIVES

The life-goal fireball is an effective, momentum-building methodology that I hope will be immensely helpful for you, but I'd be remiss if I didn't take a brief moment to talk about the weather of our lives. Every season is not going to be summer for you and me, where the sun comes out and stays out to create the perfect conditions for work and play. Sometimes it rains a little, and other times it rains so hard we can't help but wonder where all that water is coming from. You will also experience seasons where it gets bitterly cold and the ice makes travel treacherous. Weather and seasonal changes can be so unpredictable and sudden that you just don't see them coming. When this happens, know that you aren't the only person it happens to. It happens to all of us, and occasionally the fire is bound to be put out, the wood is going to be wet, and it's going to require you to regroup and refresh. This is the cycle of life, and you will need to trust that no matter how uncomfortable it feels when things fall apart, you will recover. You have endured and overcome obstacles many times before. They're never easy, but you have what it takes to survive them and live to tell the story.

> Occasionally the fire is bound to be put out, the wood is going to be wet, and it's going to require you to regroup and refresh.

If you want to conquer fear, don't sit at home and think about it.

Go out and get busy.

—DALE CARNEGIE

The secret of getting ahead is getting started.

—MARK TWAIN

Start where you are. Use what you have. Do what you can.

—ARTHUR ASHE

You can't build a reputation on what you are going to do.

—HENRY FORD

8

GO!

Create Your 100 Life Goals Now
and Make Them Public

This is not a book of theories. It's an action book. It's a workbook. At its core, it's the true definition of a self-help book. While I've spent the past seven chapters teaching you which obstacles you must overcome and how to create a master plan that brings about real change in your life, now it's your turn to take your 100 life goals and go public with them. Yes, this step is required. For some of you, the idea of going public is terrifying. I get it, but you must understand that this step is not a mere formality but an essential piece of the puzzle. Just know that as you craft your goals and go public with them, thousands of other people are going to be taking the same bold step with you. You will never be alone on this journey.

PRIVATE DREAMS ARE DEAD DREAMS

We keep our dreams to ourselves for so many deep reasons. We most often claim it's because we fear rejection and ridicule, but far more self-destructive reasons are the true culprits. When we keep our dreams and ideas and goals secret, we never feel a real burden to pursue them. Nobody can hold us responsible or accountable. By tucking our dreams away and compartmentalizing them into a secret space deep in our imagination, we give ourselves a strange sense of permission to be okay with living far beneath our potential. But there could be so much more. In fact, I believe we love real-life heroes and even comic book superheroes so much because they act on the instincts and ideas that most of us tend to ignore.

I've said it before, but it's worth repeating that the most amazing ideas and businesses and inventions and world-changing movements are far more likely to die a lonely death in our minds than they ever are at the hands of others. I can only speculate how much better our world might be if even just a small percentage of us decided to get our dreams out of our heads and into the earth. I'm not saying that we should all rashly act on every idea that crosses our minds, but if acting on every idea is foolish, ignoring every idea is just as bad, if not worse.

On May 25, 1961, President John F. Kennedy, after months of internal debating, announced that the United States was going to send a man to walk on the moon and bring him back safely before the end of the decade. Not content to simply write a press release or even announce it at a press conference, President Kennedy brought the entire United States Congress together to address them and the nation simultaneously. By pronouncing it in such a bold, public fashion, President Kennedy came forward not only to own the idea and its mission but to make it clear that he believed in it so much that he was willing to stake his name and reputation on it. Note that President Kennedy didn't just state publicly that a mission to put a man on the moon was about to begin, but he gave a specific date it needed to happen by and made it clear that a safe return home was also a part of

If acting on every idea is foolish, ignoring every idea is just as bad, if not worse.

the mission. This announcement was a YORG if I've ever heard of one; it was going to be complicated, expensive, and dangerous, and would require 1,001 other pieces (and people) to fall into place before it could happen.

President Kennedy had the forethought to see that setting a goal so audacious would force the United States to grow in ways that it only could if it pursued this dream, and he was right. The technology required to get a team of people to land on the moon, walk on it, talk to people on earth from the moon, then return home safely just didn't exist in 1961—and likely wasn't going to exist unless it became a national priority. Nobody can jump right into achieving a YORG, but instead one must marshal every resource imaginable and prepare for the years and years it will take to achieve it. By going public with this goal, President Kennedy—who would not live to see the mission fulfilled just months before his original deadline on July 20, 1969—set the United States down a path of growth and innovation that truly changed the entire trajectory of the country.

President Kennedy didn't have all the answers and knew it

would take nearly a decade for his big goal to become a reality, but he had a clear mission, an obvious target, and a deadline. Of course you and I don't have the power to convene a government body to announce our 100 life goals, but I want you to consider going public in all four of the following ways:

1. Publish your list to a friendly and encouraging audience on 100LifeGoals.com. Think of this diverse group of dreamers from all over the world as your partners in this journey. In fact, these online friends may be much easier for you to relate to and connect with than the immediate friends and family around you. It's highly likely that they've read this book and that they are having all the same fears and concerns you are having. By connecting with like-minded people, you will feel like there's always somebody somewhere who understands your highs and lows while pursuing life goals.

2. E-mail everybody you know about it in one mass e-mail. Be sure to BCC (blind carbon copy) their e-mail addresses so that replies don't get on everybody's nerves. In your e-mail, ask your network to please take a look at your list to see what they think and to consider if they may be able to partner with you on any of the goals. You may not get any responses at all, but I want you to understand that your friends, family, and coworkers may have more connections and resources to help you than you realize. Just as people don't really know your goals in life, you don't really know much about the goals and dreams of those around you

either. When you go public, you will be surprised at how many people tell you that they share your goals or know people who do.

3. Post a link to your goals on all of your social networks. The great part about social media is that it's easy for other people to share what you're doing with their own networks. Again, ask your online friends to take a look at the list to be inspired but also to see if they are able to help or partner with you on any of your goals. Even the small chance that someone can help is worth taking this risk. And don't just update your networks one time, but give regular updates on your progress as well.

4. Last—and this may be the hardest option for some of you—tell your closest friends and family members about your goals in person if you can. Using Skype or making a phone call is also an option, but it'd be great if you either convened your family together or made the effort to tell each key family member and close friend about the new direction you are going to take your life in. When you do this, do it knowing that everybody won't support it or love it, but my best guess is that at least one person is going to be inspired enough to want to take this journey with you. No matter what, the people closest to you need to understand that your days of leading a mediocre and predictable life are over.

BENEFITS OF GOING PUBLIC

Going public with your private dreams and goals is far more terrifying in your mind than it will actually feel when it happens. More times than not, the worst reaction to your public goals will be indifference, but most people will actually be supportive and excited about your boldness. The key here is to focus on the real benefits of going public versus the fears you may create in your mind. Here are a few of the key benefits:

It Extends the Life of Your Goals

When I was a kid I used to want to be an executive in the music industry. As a teenager I promoted hip-hop concerts and DJ'd parties regularly. Before I ever loved charitable work or business, I loved music and thought I could one day make a living in the industry somehow. However, for reasons I can't explain, I let go of those aspirations. I have the same story for sports. For years my dream was to become an owner or general manager of a professional sports team. As with everybody else, though, life had a weird way of talking me out of those dreams. My college major didn't really prepare me for them, and my life drifted in a different direction.

Something strange has been happening to me recently, though. Now that I'm living life without limits, the old dreams that I used to have are starting to come back to me, and I find myself wondering if I could still give them a shot. This is exactly what I want for you.

Private goals and dreams die and disappear far too easily. Writing them down at least gets them out of your head, but going public puts your goals and dreams into the minds of other people. It's hard to delete something once it has gone public. You can

> When you share them with the public, your dreams will stop being disposable and will live beyond the whims of your doubts.

always alter and tinker with your public goals, but going public breathes a new level of fresh life into them. Sometimes simply keeping your dreams and goals alive is all you need to ride out the inevitable storms and valleys. When you share them with the public, your dreams will stop being disposable and will live beyond the whims of your doubts.

It Attracts the Right Kind of People

As long as people have no idea what you want out of life, they can't help you. By going public with your goals and dreams, not only will you be more aware of the right people you need to connect with, but they will be more aware of you as well. I'm not going to get into the laws of attraction here, but I believe in them on the most basic level. What you put out in the world has a lot to do with what you get back.

Every time I express a dream or goal that I have publicly, I am shocked by the e-mails or tweets or Facebook messages that I get from people who offer encouragement, advice, insight, coaching, or more. Just recently I shared a goal I had that would require me to connect directly with an executive from Amazon. I included my e-mail with the post on the off chance that someone from Amazon might see the goal. I didn't know of anyone working there, but sure enough an online friend of mine, Stephen Matlock, wrote me back to say that he had been working for Amazon for over ten years and would advise me the best he could. Within hours of Stephen's reaching out to me, I already had a much better idea of how the goal I had would be possible.

When I expressed publicly a few years ago that I was interested in mountaineering, people came out of the woodwork telling me about their mountaineering experiences and skills. See, it's unlikely that the person next door to you is a mountaineer, but when you put it out there for the whole world to see, it *is* likely that at least one person out there is and can offer some valuable insight or advice on how you can be successful. Since I first posted this goal, I've had people offer to guide me for free on mountains in South America and even had a company offer to pay me to help lead a team climbing Mount Kilimanjaro in Tanzania, Africa. I have a hundred more stories like this and hear them almost daily from my clients. The people around you, either in person or online, are some of the greatest untapped resources of your life.

It Attracts the Right Kind of Resources

I used to be the type of guy who wondered why good things always seemed to happen to certain people and not others. In fact, I used to think that good things unfairly seemed to happen to the same people over and over again, and I didn't understand why. While the sophisticated truth may require delving into a conversation about socioeconomics, I want to suggest something altogether different that truly transcends race, class, and gender in so many ways. When you make up your mind to pursue your dreams and go public with them, doors will open. I'm not saying that *every* door is going to open, but *some* will. You will undoubtedly still have to knock down other doors, but unless you take this step, you won't even know where those are to knock them down in the first place.

I recently expressed on social media that I was interested in earning my PhD. I'm still on the fence about it, but it has always been a dream of mine that I've kept to myself. I'd love to teach and lead at the university level someday. Almost every day since I wrote that post, people have reached out to me with insightful tips, suggestions of books, and more. Yet other people have told me they don't even think I need to get a PhD and could do whatever I needed to do without such a degree. Either way, my act of going public started to open up a whole new world for me that will help me make an informed decision in the months ahead.

As long as your dreams and goals are private, you'll find yourself constantly missing out on free and valuable resources that are out there waiting for you. By going public, not only will friends and family be keeping their eyes open for all kinds of deals to help you accomplish your goals, but you will also be on the radar of companies and experts you will need along the way. Remember that the first two to three steps for each goal are always free and help you to get the basic education and connections you need to make them happen.

It Provides Healthy Peer Pressure

I'm all for having a few trade secrets and even holding a few cards close to your chest, but once you go public with your life goals, people are going to start asking you how you're doing and if you have any hard-core updates. This level of performance peer pressure will cause you to work harder to have good news to report back to your network. As a general rule, it's preferable to surround yourself with friends and family members who genuinely want you to grow and become your best self. The flip side of that is also true: when you are surrounded by people who either don't care about your growth or, worse, actively discourage you from growing, they influence you to go down paths of negativity. This makes it nearly impossible for you to get ahead in life.

A few years ago I was a part of a mountaineering team climbing Mount Rainier. Without a doubt, I was the weakest, most inexperienced person on the team. Beyond the fact that I arrived with a terrible sinus infection and was taking antibiotics the whole trip, I just wasn't in the condition I needed to be in. The leaders of my expedition did something that I'll never forget. Instead of putting me at the very back of our climbing line, they put me in between the two best climbers on our twelve-person team. The person in front of me would set the pace, and the person behind me would encourage me verbally and keep a strong pace as well. For the next ten hours of climbing, I knew that if I slowed down I'd disappoint the teammate behind me and distract the teammate who was leading the way. At times I felt like I was going to die trying to keep up, but I got the point. The pressure of being between two great climbers caused me to push myself to the max. I'm convinced that I wouldn't have made it even halfway up Mount Rainier without being pushed and pulled by my peers every foot of the way.

While healthy peer pressure can be a good thing, I do want to caution you against allowing it to dictate your every move. Sometimes you are going to have to make decisions that few people will understand or appreciate. I regularly take somewhat controversial stands on issues such as racism or human trafficking. Without fail, almost every time I speak my mind, someone who loves me asks if I'm rocking the boat too much. While I'll admit that from time to time I rock the boat so much that it's more like wrecking the ship, I do so because I have a core value to speak out on certain issues even if doing so isn't popular. When the 276 rural schoolgirls in Chibok, Nigeria, were kidnapped, I spoke out so hard and so often that my tweets on the topic were among the most shared in the world for the first few weeks. Daily somebody offered a snide remark on why I cared so much and asked me if I really thought my tweets would make a difference. In this instance, I felt like I was going against the grain of peer pressure to stand up for what I thought was right, and eventually the tide turned with me. Even if the tide doesn't turn, you have to be willing to go against the grain and take calculated risks to pursue the things that matter the most to you.

It Sets Higher Expectations

Growing up in Versailles, Kentucky, I was a huge fan of the University of Kentucky men's basketball team. While other teams are happy to make it to the NCAA tournament, anything short of a championship at Kentucky has a way of feeling like a disappointment. The collective expectations are so high that the players, coaches, and staff know they must rise to the occasion. Other teams believe in the moral victory of making it to the Final Four, but the Kentucky Wildcats are always fighting for first place. I've seen the same culture of high expectations with the Los Angeles Lakers. They've won a dozen NBA championships since the 1980s, so you'll never see the Lakers celebrating after a first- or second-round play-off victory, because the team expects better than that every year.

In the same way, private dreams have a way of keeping your expectations incredibly low in life. When you go public, it's a crucial first step to having higher expectations for yourself, which is always a key to success. The best companies and leaders in the world get great, and stay that way, because they have such high standards. Low expectations are self-fulfilling prophecies. When you expect to fail or flop, you almost always do. When you expect to succeed, you may not always hit your mark, but it's way more likely you'll come close trying. Outside of the lottery, rarely will you hear winners of anything of note tell you they prepared for failure in their minds. That's not to say that success will never be sweet or even surprising, but when you have high expectations it will be much less rare.

Low expectations are self-fulfilling prophecies.

SURPRISE BLESSINGS

As you pursue the most ambitious goals of your life, you are going to need every break and advantage you can get. While many of these will be created as a result of your own hard work, going public with your goals, perhaps more than any other action, opens up the possibility of surprise blessings. The truth is that as long as you keep your best ambitions to yourself, friends and family who may want to support you, as well as strangers who may somehow identify with your pursuits and want to become partners, are all denied the opportunity to do so. While miraculous surprises can't be guaranteed, I can assure you that you will all but eliminate their appearance if you keep your dreams to yourself.

PART C

THE SEVEN INTERLOCKING LIFE-GOAL CATEGORIES

Lifting Up Your Entire Life

Our deepest fear is not that we are inadequate. Our deepest fear is that we are powerful beyond measure.

—MARIANNE WILLIAMSON

There are no extra pieces in the universe. Everyone is here because he or she has a place to fill, and every piece must fit itself into the big jigsaw puzzle.

—DEEPAK CHOPRA

To live is the rarest thing in the world. Most people exist, that is all.

—OSCAR WILDE

For most of my adult life I operated off the strength and momentum of my primary skills and gifts. I've been speaking to large crowds and coming up with witty ideas since I was seventeen. Consequently, almost everything I did for the first ten years I was out on my own revolved around the skills of public speaking and developing fresh ideas. Don't get me wrong, those two gifts opened up a lot of doors, but it took me hitting a few walls and glass ceilings to realize that my baseline gifts couldn't keep the doors open. Time and time again, when an idea that had launched off the momentum of my core skills required me to be bigger or better or deeper than those skills, my momentum stalled. It stumped me, because I had poured out everything I had, giving maximum effort to making my dreams succeed.

I saw it when I was student government president at Morehouse College. I saw it when I started Courageous Church in inner-city Atlanta. I definitely saw it when I started TwitChange, HopeMob, and Upfront, my first businesses in the tech world. I was great at busting an opportunity wide open and even at getting it off the ground, but I simply lacked the diverse set of skills and depth needed to take really good ideas and grow them into truly great businesses and charities.

Anybody could argue for the addition or subtraction of one or two of the interlocking life-goal categories that I am teaching you. However, I've found from my own successes and failures, and all the research that I have done studying some of the most successful people in history, that if you can have a baseline of competence in all seven of these areas—not necessarily mastery, but at least a working competence—it will not only lift the low ceiling of your potential, but it will open up opportunities you never before thought possible.

Read each of the following seven chapters for motivation and guidance as you carefully fine-tune all 100 of your life goals. If you find that you already have a real strength in one of the categories, don't blow through it, but begin to imagine how you can harness your strengths and make them work better for you. Plan on making the areas of your life where you are competent but not great into true areas of strength.

Finally, my dream for you is something that I am personally working on every single day. It doesn't come easy, but the difference maker is going to be taking your weaknesses and liabilities and turning them into areas where you are at least average but are also improving daily. Of course I can't guarantee that you'll never hit another wall, but I can say with real confidence that you won't hit one because of a huge area you've been avoiding. You'll still need as much luck and good timing as the next person, but I have a feeling that if you develop this plan and work it like your life depends on it, you're going to start feeling like the luckiest person alive.

Do all the good you can,

By all the means you can,

In all the ways you can,

In all the places you can,

At all the times you can,

To all the people you can,

As long as ever you can.

—JOHN WESLEY

If you can't feed a hundred people, then feed just one.

—MOTHER TERESA

First they came for the communists, and I did not speak out—

because I was not a communist;

Then they came for the socialists, and I did not speak out—

because I was not a socialist;

Then they came for the trade unionists, and I did not speak out—

because I was not a trade unionist;

Then they came for the Jews, and I did not speak out—

because I was not a Jew;

Then they came for me—

and there was no one left to speak out for me.

—MARTIN NIEMÖLLER

9

GENEROSITY GOALS

How Will I Make the World a Better Place?

As far as I'm concerned, any life plan kicked off by generosity is already on the right track.

Completely absent from far too many bucket lists are ways that we can ease the suffering of others and make the world a better place. John Goddard, often called the real-life Indiana Jones and the father of life-goal lists, wrote down 100 life goals when he was just fifteen years old in 1940. For the next seventy years he accomplished all but two or three of them and is generally thought to be one of the greatest adventurers of the twentieth century. I admire him a great deal. The problem, though, with a fifteen-year-old boy writing a bucket list is that it is more than likely about as selfish as the average teenager is. Reflecting back on life before he passed away in 2013, Goddard said he wished his goals had done more to include family and generosity. The limitations of his list and the way bucket lists have been made ever since are a huge reason why I'm doing it differently. Generosity and compassion aren't just good for the world; they are good for your soul.

In the years that I've been teaching people to set and pursue 100 life goals, I've always found that not only does starting off with generosity awaken your heart, but generosity goals flow out so easily that they're a great way to have momentum from day one. Most of us can think of dozens and dozens of ways we'd like to see the world improve in our hometown, in our state, in our country, and certainly all over the world. Perhaps the most beautiful thing about being generous is that we always begin acts of generosity hoping to use our time, money, skills, and influence to make the world a better place, but we end up being enriched from the inside out more than we could ever imagine.

Soon after the devastating earthquake hit Haiti in 2010, I started raising money online and organizing relief teams from Atlanta to help however we could. On my first visit I went to rural Haiti to a home for disabled children—many of them orphaned by the earthquake. I was honestly not prepared for what I saw. Living in the poorest area of the poorest country in the Western Hemisphere, these children, sometimes with terminal illnesses or severe disabilities that prevented them from walking or talking, were the happiest, sweetest kids I had ever met. I don't think even one of the kids I spent time with was able to speak a single word to me, but they smiled and laughed and wanted to hold hands or have me pick them up and hold them or carry them any time they saw me. I had come there to see how I could pitch in and help, but my experience of pure joy with those babies did way more for me than I ever did for them.

After I returned home to my own family, I immediately began telling my wife she had to go and see these wonderful children for herself. The mistake I made, though, was telling her every detail of just how rough the flights and drives and living conditions were. My wife's a tough woman, but back then she had never traveled outside of the country and was far from excited about the idea of roughing it. After I convinced nearly fifty other people to take the trip with me, Rai finally decided she'd come, too. Once we landed in Port-au-Prince, I started thinking I had made a huge mistake inviting her. It was chaos inside the airport, and it was ten times worse outside. For every five feet we walked, someone, likely in legitimate need, asked us for money. Taxi drivers begged us to get in their cars. It was over 100 degrees and about as dusty as a place could ever be.

We got into the back of a pickup truck and drove to another small airport, where we waited for about three hours for our next flight, to the rural northwest town of Saint-Louis-du-Nord. My wife was not pleased. When we finally walked out to the plane and boarded, it was already packed with luggage and boxes, so we found the last two seats available in the back. I had told Rai how beautiful Haiti was and how precious the kids were, but so far she was only seeing the worst. She wasn't talking to me by this point, and it ended up getting much worse. The plane didn't have air-conditioning, so we were drenched in sweat. As we prepared for takeoff, the pilot, who wasn't behind a security door or anything, turned around and told us that once we were in the air he'd open some windows to get a breeze going.

For the next hour, it seemed like the engine completely cut off at least four times, and we plummeted a few hundred feet every time it happened. Clearly on the verge of either vomiting or killing me, my wife kept a death grip on my hand that I've only seen happen with women in labor on television. I tried to reassure her, but to be perfectly honest, I also thought we might die on that plane. It was that bad. I'm usually known to have nerves of steel, but I was secretly praying to God the entire time. Even though the flight was just an hour long, it felt like ten. As we finally came in for a landing on the dusty airstrip in rural Haiti, we narrowly missed some goats strolling carelessly on the runway. I thought my wife was going to leave me. I had not told her that the car ride for the next ninety minutes was also likely going to be the worst she had ever been on. It was.

By the time we arrived where we were staying, at the headquarters of the charity that was hosting us, her nerves were shot. The rough living conditions, terrible restrooms, and nearly inedible meals only made things worse. Instead of slowly introducing my wife to international aid, I had just given her a one-day crash course in some of the worst conditions possible during the hardest time Haiti had ever seen. When we woke up the next morning, though, I think she was so glad just to be alive and safe that she truly seemed like a brand-new woman. After breakfast, she and I were introduced to the sweetest, cutest little girl, named Rachel. A mother at heart, my wife melted. Rachel was probably three to four years old, but she wasn't much bigger than an eighteen-month-old baby. With an undiagnosed neurological disorder, she could not walk, talk, or move any part of her body. All she could really do was smile, and it was enough. Rai and I were hooked. The brutal trip became a distant memory, and we spent the better part of the next few days holding and loving on Rachel.

Her sweetness tugged at our hearts so much that Rai and I inquired about adopting her, but she wasn't available for adoption. Undeterred, we seriously considered moving our entire family to rural Haiti just so we could be there to love and take care of Rachel. By "seriously considered," I mean we talked out the details of what it would take, when we could do it, and how we could close our business in the States to make it work. What we thought was going to be a simple trip where we'd volunteer here and there and serve where we could turned out to be something much deeper and life-changing. Our minds raced with ideas about how we could pull off something so radical. Our hearts were open in ways we had never experienced. The suffering of a little child with a tender soul and a million-dollar smile broke us all the way down.

It was then that the true power of generosity crystallized in my mind. When you truly give, without pretense or expectation, but just to serve, you open up your heart to be blessed in immeasurable and unpredictable ways. Of all my memories of world travel— hanging out with celebrities, winning awards, speaking to huge crowds, starting and selling businesses—all of them pale in comparison with holding little Rachel and having her look up and smile from ear to ear. In those moments, Mother Teresa made sense to us. Giving everything you own away and simply loving suffering kids has a way of fulfilling you more than material goods or applause ever will, and it's something that you have to experience for yourself.

A life grounded in generosity is a life well lived.

A life grounded in generosity is a life well lived. While my expressed goal is for you to have as balanced a life as humanly possible, I want to level with you—getting these generosity goals well crafted and in motion is my highest priority for you. If you open your mind to the particular ways you want to make the world a better place, you will soon find that pursuing these goals will instill a hunger to be better in every other area of your life as well in order to make your giving possible. For instance, I know that if I want to free 100,000 people caught up in modern-day slavery, I not only need to travel but will need a flexible career, a good budget, strong health, a supportive family, inner strength, and more. I am much more likely to be motivated to be physically fit and financially secure if I'm driven by something like freeing people from human trafficking than I ever would be by the desire to look like a supermodel or show off like a rapper.

Below I'm going to get you started. Remember, each goal needs to be concise and measurable, and it needs to fit within the framework we talked about earlier to help you build momentum. As always, visit 100LifeGoals.com for motivation, training, and a lively community of people on this same journey with you.

LIFE-GOAL TEMPLATE

✓ Generosity YORG

✓ Two goals you can complete within two months. They should be close to free and be at least loosely related to your YORG.

✓ Three goals you can complete within one year. They should increase in commitment and cost, and some should be related to your YORG.

✓ Five goals that will take one to five years each. They should increase in commitment and cost, and some should be related to your YORG.

✓ Two goals that will absolutely take more than five years to achieve. These are almost YORGs. One should be related to your YORG.

Most people work hard and spend their health trying to achieve wealth. Then they retire and spend their wealth trying to get back their health.

—KEVIN GIANNI

Health is a state of complete harmony of the body, mind, and spirit. When one is free from physical disabilities and mental distractions, the gates of the soul open.

—B. K. S. IYENGAR

Our bodies are our gardens—our wills are our gardeners.

—WILLIAM SHAKESPEARE

10

HEALTH AND FITNESS GOALS

How Will I Give My Body the Best Chance?

I was a pretty athletic kid. I was skinny as a rail, but I don't remember a tired day in my entire childhood. I played baseball and some soccer, dabbled in wrestling and karate, ran track, and was in the high school marching band. I didn't know it until I got my first car, but my friends and I would often ride our bikes as much as ten miles a day. There were times when we went the same distances walking and never complained. I didn't have the type of abs that you'd see on the front of a magazine, but I had a flat stomach with enough definition for a teenage boy to think he was hot stuff.

Everything about my physical life changed on March 8, 1995. I was a sophomore at Woodford County High School in my small hometown of Versailles, Kentucky. For the year and a half of high school before that day, I had been harassed almost daily by a growing group of self-proclaimed rednecks. I had been forced into fights, had all my books and belongings thrown into the trash, been called every ugly racist name imaginable, been chased and nearly run over by a pickup truck, and even had a full jar of tobacco spit thrown in my face. On more than one occasion cars came to my house in the middle of the night and peeled out in my yard. I was constantly under the threat of attack. The bottom finally fell out on that spring day in 1995.

Standing near the gym with my friends before my eleven a.m. band class down the hall, we saw a large crowd of about twenty-five students in what looked like a fight that had just ended. Fights were a regular thing in my high school and broke out at any random moment. Leron Clark, a good buddy of mine who lived just a few blocks away from me, leaned over to comment on how tired he was of there always being somebody fighting. I smiled, agreed, and decided to walk on to band class before the bell rang. I had to walk through that gathered crowd to get to my class but really didn't think anything of it. The closer I got to the crowd, though, the stranger it seemed. What was once an active, bustling, even rowdy group of teenagers had grown silent. Had I known that I was about to enter into the wolf's den, I would have turned around.

"There he is. That's Shaun King," said a faceless male voice.

"Yep. That's him," said another.

Completely naive about what was about to happen, I kept on walking but noticed that it was getting harder and harder to push my way through the cluster of bodies that had stiffened up around me. About midway through, I felt a heavy thud on the back of my head. In an instant the crowd swarmed me and started punching from every angle. What felt like an hour but was probably more like fifteen seconds passed before I fell to the ground. Stomped from my face to my feet with steel-toed boots, I heard voices laughing at my broken body as I involuntarily curled up into the fetal position.

As a few of my fellow classmates pushed their way through and found me a bloody mess on the floor, the mob dispersed and I was physically ruined. With fractures in my face and ribs, permanently injured sinuses, and a severely damaged spine, I missed the next year and a half of high school recovering from three of the most miserable spinal surgeries ever. Needless to say, my body never fully mended. Four years after I was assaulted I had to be carried out of my college dorm room for yet another emergency spinal surgery for the same injuries. In the nearly fifteen years that have passed since that last surgery, I've been in some kind of pain every day of my life. Pain became my new normal. The car crash that I was in, as you can imagine, didn't make it any easier.

On the average day now, everything in my body tells me to find a quiet place to put my feet up, do my work, and try not to make my body hurt any more than it already does. I wasn't always this way, but my strong inclination, almost daily, is to get in bed and rest. This is about the worst equation for physical fitness known to man. However, I am keenly aware that if I am going to accomplish even half of my 100 life goals, I can't be sedentary, overweight, or out of shape.

While it may indeed be unlikely that health and fitness will become the highest-performing area of my life, it's up to me, daily, to make sure I have a core competence and give my body every chance it can get to succeed. For me this means avoiding unhealthy foods like the plague; eating clean, healthy, and whole snacks and meals; and ignoring the pain all over my body by pushing through and being as active as possible. On a bad day that may mean just getting out of bed, stretching a little, and walking around the house. Because the days I feel great are so rare, when they do come, I make sure I use them to be at my physical best by walking, hiking, going to the beach with the family, playing with the kids, or even going grocery shopping with my wife. I'm also the coach of my son's Little League baseball team, and his practice, no matter what pain I'm in, requires me to be very active every Thursday at four p.m. Setting up recurring appointments like this forces me to push myself outside of my comfort zone and simply works well for me.

It helps to know that so many other people have also pushed through physical disabilities to achieve greatness.

Fully blind, Stevie Wonder has recorded thirty top 10 hits.

Completely deaf, Marlee Matlin has won both an Academy Award and a Golden Globe.

Franklin Delano Roosevelt, paralyzed from the waist down, guided America through World War II and is generally thought to be one of the best American presidents ever.

Deaf and blind, Helen Keller found a way to be a prolific author and antiwar activist, and met every American president from Grover Cleveland to Lyndon Johnson.

I share these stories not to prepare you for a time when you have a disability but to encourage you with the idea that if they can push through, so can you. Hopefully, you never suffer from severe health challenges, but wherever you are on the spectrum of health and fitness, you must discover what specialized plan of action works for you, what keeps you motivated in a society that pushes poor health on you from every side, who can coach and guide you along the journey, and what goals you can set that will take your physical life to the next level.

YOUR MOST PREVENTABLE ROADBLOCK

As you craft and pursue your 100 life goals, many unforeseen road-blocks will attempt to derail you and throw you completely off course. Perhaps nothing has the power to rock your entire world like a health crisis. It can crush you financially, put an enormous strain on your family, and quickly spiral into the primary focus of your life. While some diseases and ailments are seemingly random and have little to do with your choices, study after study shows us that the decisions we make to eat well, stay fit, get good sleep, manage our stress, and avoid drugs and negative relationships will virtually eliminate many cancers, heart disease, every STD, high blood pressure, diabetes, hypertension, and so much more. One hundred percent of the world will tell you that they don't want any of those ailments, but the truth is we are giving them to ourselves. The correlation between our poor choices and our poor health is about as proven as gravity, yet we live like one is fact and one is fic-tion, and do so at our own peril.

Having an incredibly healthy life will give you a much better chance to fight off diseases, ailments, and injuries. The reverse of that is also true. If we happen to get injured or sick and are already in poor health, our ability to recover is greatly diminished, and what could have been a short setback can end up turning into a full-blown crisis. Once you have diabetes or heart disease or a preventable form of cancer, the effects and the treatment have a way of taking over. Saying stupid stuff like "We're all going to die one day anyway" or "We all have to die somehow" is a lame excuse for living in a way that unnecessarily ruins the quality of your life, negatively impacts those around you, and prevents you from achieving your goals and dreams.

YOUR MOST AFFORDABLE AND MOST REWARDING GOALS

Physical fitness and overall health are not expensive goals beyond your reach. We tell ourselves they are so that we can maintain the comfortable lifestyles of our poor decisions, but of all the seven life-goal categories, this one can be the most affordable and the most rewarding. While I accept that the willpower and discipline required here are pretty epic if you're going to see results, you have everything you need to get started today.

It doesn't cost a dime for you to walk or run a mile in the morning and a mile in the evening and gradually kick those up a small notch every day.

It doesn't cost you a dime to wake up and do aerobics or yoga with a training video on YouTube.

Eating a piece of fruit and a bowl of oatmeal with a cool glass of water from home in the morning will cost you less time and money than a tall mocha latte and a blueberry muffin from Starbucks.

Even buying P90X or a monthly online membership to one of

the amazing Internet-based fitness training programs will cost you less per month than one visit to the movies or subscribing to HBO.

The rewards, though, for making the small financial investment in your health and fitness are endless and better experienced than read. You will have more energy, less stress, and better self-esteem, and you will begin to consider goals and risks that you would never have considered when you ignored your health and fitness. For instance, my wife, who

You have everything you need to get started today.

is a workout beast, is now talking about climbing Mount Rainier outside of Seattle with me in the future. I'm blown away by that, because I remember so many times in the past when she told me she'd never do such a thing. Her fitness has given her a bold sense of confidence to try new things that will push her mind and body to another level.

LIFE-GOAL TEMPLATE

✓ Health and Fitness YORG

✓ Two goals you can complete within two months. They should be close to free and be at least loosely related to your YORG.

✓ Three goals you can complete within one year. They should increase in commitment and cost, and some should be related to your YORG.

✓ Five goals that will take one to five years each. They should increase in commitment and cost, and some should be related to your YORG.

✓ Two goals that will absolutely take more than five years to achieve. These are almost YORGs. One should be related to your YORG.

The worst days of those who enjoy what they
do are better than the best days of those who don't.

—JAMES ROHN

If you follow your bliss, you put yourself on a kind of track,
which has been there all the while waiting for you, and the life
that you ought to be living is the one you are living.

—JOSEPH CAMPBELL

When you are inspired by some great purpose, some
extraordinary project, all your thoughts break their bounds.
Your mind transcends limitations, your consciousness expands
in every direction and you find yourself in a new, great and
wonderful world. Dormant forces, faculties and talents become
alive, and you discover yourself to be a greater person by far
than you ever dreamed yourself to be.

—PATANJALI

11

CAREER AND FINANCE GOALS

How Can I Find Financial Freedom
While Doing What I Love?

When the people you most deeply admire are modern-day legends like Dr. King, Mother Teresa, Nelson Mandela, and Gandhi, something very confusing can happen. As you seek to become like those men and women in terms of the impact they made on the world—and I certainly do—you can accidentally overstudy the impact they made toward the end of their lives at the expense of studying the 1,001 very difficult and deliberate steps they took before they were doing the work we know them for.

We study Dr. King and his amazing speeches before crowds large and small or see his bravery in the face of people who wanted him dead or in jail, and we wonder how we can make an impact like that. Don't get me wrong, that's fine, but in studying the culmination of his activism, we forget that ten years before Dr. King told us about his dream, he toiled away almost anonymously in Boston, earning his PhD.

We study Mahatma Gandhi and see what looks like a feeble warrior, bald, shoeless, shirtless, toothless, simple, a little guru with glasses, and we're blown away by the idea that such a man could stand up and lead a revolt against colonialism in his country. In reducing the man to a symbol, we miss that he had been a fierce attorney fighting for civil and human rights in South Africa for decades before the world knew his name. Before he ever wrapped himself in a flowing white robe and became a global icon, he wore three-piece suits and argued before judges in courts of law. In fact, he was nearly fifty years old before he moved back to India after being educated in London and having a twenty-one-year law career in South Africa.

It's a beautiful thing that the world knows and loves Nelson Mandela. Probably the last true globally revered political leader before he passed away in 2014, Mandela was a senior citizen by the time he was elected president of South Africa in 1994. Not only had he spent twenty-eight years of his life in prison, but he, like Gandhi before him, had been a well-educated attorney and full-fledged freedom fighter in South Africa long before the world knew his name.

Born in 1910 as Gonxha Agnes Bojaxhiu in Skopje, Macedonia, Mother Teresa is known today for her compassionate love of the kids of Calcutta, India, suffering the effects of severe poverty and disease. Nearly forty years old before she began to serve the poor full-time, Mother Teresa said that there were nearly ten years, from 1949 to 1959, in which she had severe doubts that God even existed and that she had lost faith altogether during that time. Now, after a lifetime of service to the poor, she is known for her unwavering trust in God and ability to serve the poor in the hardest circumstances imaginable. Her early doubts did not derail her from her greater purpose.

I lift these examples up to show you that there are no true shortcuts to success. The path is a long, winding, and often unpredictable one. Without fail, the most admired and respected people in the world paid their dues for years and years before they had the impact that we know them for. Mother Teresa was a teacher and missionary for twenty years before she began her life's work, but she had put herself in such a position of respect that when she was ready to form her own mission to serve the poor it was quickly approved by the Vatican. Dr. King, Nelson Mandela, and Gandhi all stated that education opened up doors for them that would have otherwise been closed. Of course, courage and determination gave them the strength to walk through the doors, but without the PhDs and law degrees that laid the groundwork before they became household names, it's likely that those leaders would not have broken through the way they did.

TAKE THE LONG VIEW

My broader point is not an argument for extensive formal education but to say that it often takes years, decades even, of very focused, hard work before you are going to see the results you dream of with your career, finances, and impact. When you are willing to take the long view, it opens a brand-new world of possibilities, but even with that long view, you must take steps today to begin cultivating your dream for next year or ten or twenty years from now. To prepare to become president of the United States, one doesn't become a presidential historian but typically gets a law or business degree, works in the private sector, then eventually becomes a governor or US senator. What I'm getting at is that the path to success in a particular career may not even be studying that career but having great success elsewhere. Oprah Winfrey, for instance, has started one of the best schools for girls in the world, but her path there didn't include her becoming a public or private school principal.

I have a dream that I can't shake to start a creative and performing arts middle and high school in downtown Atlanta. The vision for it made a lot more sense when I lived in Atlanta, but even now that I've left and moved all over the world, the dream remains. For me, the abiding sense that won't go away is one clue that I should at least investigate it. When I first conceived the dream, my oldest children were still in elementary school, and I wasn't sure they'd ever be interested in such a place. Lo and behold, our daughter Kendi just got accepted into one of the best performing arts schools in the country, and I'm going to use my time as a caring parent to study what makes her school so successful. It could be years and years before I attempt to start a school in Atlanta, but I'm finding small ways today to make that dream just a little more possible. Even my desire to grow my base of influence on social media and in the worlds of charity and technology is privately influenced by my hope to one day start this school if I so choose. This faraway dream influences the books I read, the conferences I attend, the people I follow online. Even mentioning the dream to you now is me trying to win you over to my team to one day support it!

Another long-term goal my wife and I have is paying off all of our debt, including student loans and car notes, down to a zero balance. Bit by bit, debt by debt, we're getting there. We won't be done this year or next year. It may take seven to ten years depending on our income, but if we want to be debt-free in seven years, we can't delay and must act now. Because we don't want our kids to be one day saddled with $100,000 in student loan debt of their own, we're keeping our eyes on the future and pushing them very hard academically and socially so that they will get accepted into great colleges with good offers. We are also saving money, albeit not as much as we'd like, to help them later when they may need it. Admittedly, our youngest kids may benefit from our savings more than our older ones, but at least we're on that path. Ultimately, because we have a clear vision for our future, it greatly informs our decisions and actions now.

POSITION YOURSELF TO DO WHAT YOU LOVE

It's so easy to be blinded by the job you do now and what you're trained in and have the skills to do that it can be hard to imagine doing something different in the future. If you love what you do for a living now, you are in a shockingly small minority and should be grateful. If you are in that ever-growing majority of people thankful to have a job but frustrated by it at the same time, you need to understand that you still have time to make a dramatic shift into something altogether different. Outside of a few careers that may require you to be a certain young age, you can still put yourself on a path to becoming the person you always dreamed of being, and eventually most people won't even remember what you used to do.

I'm blessed, because more than at any other point in my life, I know today who I am, who I'm not, what makes me tick, what I love, how and where I work well, when I'm fulfilled, etc. It wasn't easy getting to this point, but as a full-time writer, executive coach, and consultant, I love what I do. I'm only doing what I do now, including writing this book, because I love it. Yes, I need the income that I get from my work, but I choose to do what I do because it gives me great satisfaction to help guide people through life. In getting to this point I experimented in many other fields before I found what I think is the intersection between what I do well, what I love doing, and what can provide for my big family. Now that I'm in that sweet spot, I find that I do my best work and make the most money doing it.

> I'm not going to *accidentally* have drastic increases in income or savings.

However—and this is a big however—I have real ambitions that go beyond that. I hope to always do what I do now, but I know that if I ever want to become president of Morehouse College or mayor of Atlanta or owner of a professional sports team (or two), then I will have to grow into new roles and opportunities down the road. In other words, what I'm doing right now is exactly what I'm supposed to be doing right now and will likely be

right for years to come, but one day—and I will know it organically when it comes—I will have to make some adjustments to
how I use my time and energy if my dreams and goals are actually
going to happen.

Just as giving a speech at the Lincoln Memorial doesn't make
you anything like Dr. Martin Luther King, doing what I do today
won't make you much like me either. We all have unique life
paths. This is why I want you to take your time when you craft
your YORG and long-term goals in this category. In order to
be able to honestly consider what steps you need to take today,
tomorrow, next month, and even next year with your career and
with your finances, you will need to add some clarity and definition to your dreams for five to forty years from now. That's not
easy to consider, but it's worth it.

FUNDING YOUR DREAMS

I'll be frank with you. I simply cannot afford 70 of my 100 life
goals. Let me clarify that a bit. *Today*, I simply cannot afford 70
of my 100 life goals. One of the main reasons I call them life goals
is because some of them will take a lifetime to accomplish. Eventually, I will need to have a significantly higher income than I do
today if many of my most ambitious goals are going to be anything
more than pipe dreams. What I am keenly aware of, though, is
this: I'm not going to *accidentally* have drastic increases in income
or savings. Those changes, as much as any I will have in my life,
will come as a result of my hard work, planning, and financial dis-

cipline. The same is true for you. Do not be discouraged by what is (or isn't) in your bank account today. Instead, as you craft the goals in this category, put yourself on an aggressive path to career, income, and investment growth. Few things in your life will need more deliberate, meticulous care than this.

LIFE-GOAL TEMPLATE

✓ Career and Finance YORG

✓ Two goals you can complete within two months. They should be close to free and be at least loosely related to your YORG.

✓ Three goals you can complete within one year. They should increase in commitment and cost, and some should be related to your YORG.

✓ Five goals that will take one to five years each. They should increase in commitment and cost, and some should be related to your YORG.

✓ Two goals that will absolutely take more than five years to achieve. These are almost YORGs. One should be related to your YORG.

Worry does not empty tomorrow of its sorrow;

it empties today of its strength.

—CORRIE TEN BOOM

I don't think of all the misery, but of the beauty that still remains.

—ANNE FRANK

Faith is taking the first step, even when you

don't see the whole staircase.

—DR. MARTIN LUTHER KING JR.

12

SPIRITUAL AND EMOTIONAL GOALS

What Will Foster Internal Strength?

I'm fully aware that half of you reading this book may not be even a little religious. This isn't the chapter where I tell you how much you need my religion, or any religion at all for that matter. That's really for you to decide. However, I can absolutely assure you that if you neglect your inner life in the pursuit of all your other life goals, you'll hit a wall early in your journey. Determination, discipline, happiness, joy, courage, tenacity, patience, wisdom, focus, clarity, and a willingness to learn are just a few of the essential traits you will need in this pursuit, and every single one of them emanates from your mind (others may say they come from your heart or soul, but you get the point). Your inner life is the engine that will push, guide, and direct you, and if you neglect it, it will break down and leave you stranded in the middle of nowhere. But if you overcome all of your emotional baggage, cultivate inner disciplines, and work hard to have a healthy thought life, you will find yourself truly free in this world, inside and out.

I can't explain why adversity breaks some people down while it builds character in other people, strengthening their resolve. The latter has been my story. All the hard times and low moments I've been through had a way of making me into the man I am today. I do struggle, though, with an over-reliance (bordering on ignorant arrogance) on my inner strength to take me places where I honestly need a whole set of skills beyond simple determination.

On my first attempt to climb Mount Rainier, my physical fitness level, while pretty good for me, was severely lacking for the brutality of the climb. Making matters worse, I had camped out with my family for several days beforehand, and I was exhausted and battling a sinus infection, already beat down physically before I even began climbing. However, I was still confident about my inner strength, sure that I could climb to the top and back safely. Nothing was going to stop me. I had convinced myself that whatever my body was lacking I would make up for in sheer will-power. It was a ruthless first day. The grueling climb had taken every ounce of physical strength I had, and we weren't even close to the top. On day two we had to traverse rocky terrain and make our way up to a glacier on the mountain at about 12,000 feet. To say that I made it to the glacier on day two is not quite true. By the time I got there, I was a hollow shell of myself and still had to set up camp. Instead of going to sleep that night, the team decided to suit up and push

> Your inner life is the engine that will push, guide, and direct you, and if you neglect it, it will break down and leave you stranded in the middle of nowhere.

for the summit at one a.m. to beat the crowd. I made it 1,000 vertical feet higher before my guide finally forced me to turn around and go back to camp. I was a complete zombie and was slowing everybody else down.

My mental fortitude had climbed 13,000 feet higher than my body was capable of climbing, but I learned a tough lesson that day. While inner strength is key to success, it works even better when coupled with physical fitness and good health. I decided from that point forward that I would only undertake such a risky endeavor again if my mind, body, and spirit were on the same level.

Far too often, though, people climb mountains with the reverse of what I had during my expedition. Armed with impeccable physical fitness but no true mental readiness, climbers often fall to their deaths, because they overestimate what their fitness alone can accomplish. Ed Viesturs, my mountaineering hero, tells the story of a buff man in tennis shoes with no climbing gear who literally attempted to run as fast as he could up Mount Rainier. Ed—perhaps the most accomplished mountaineer in the world, known for taking a steady, methodical pace—was shocked, because the man was running a full-blown sprint up the mountain. About forty-five minutes later Ed heard a loud yell. The man, with little experience or training and without the proper gear, had fallen and was now a bloody mess rocketing down the ice at an unnatural speed. His body slammed into rocks, and he died then and there—leaving a terrible red trail down the entire mountain. Mountaineering forces those who are ill prepared to pay a severe cost, and this man clearly had not thought things through.

INNER DISCIPLINES

All of us have a core set of outer disciplines that guide our physical life. We brush our teeth in the morning and at night. We eat breakfast, lunch, and dinner. Most of us sleep at night and work during the day. We change into new clothes daily. Those things are all pretty universal and represent just a small percentage of our daily physical disciplines. We learn them from a young age, and they travel with us everywhere we go. If anything, these habits should show you that you have the ability to maintain daily disciplines.

Inner disciplines for your mind, heart, and soul are equally, if not more, important but are virtually ignored by most. Prayer or meditation is an inner discipline. A few minutes of focused deep breathing in the morning is an inner discipline. A daily period of reflective gratitude for all that is good in your life and in the world is an inner discipline. Silently repeating strong affirmations or reciting sacred texts about your potential and place in the world is an inner discipline. Choosing to let go of the grip of a painful past is an inner discipline. All of these will help you be your very best throughout the day and must be repeated often.

HEALTHY THOUGHT LIFE

I'm sure you've heard it before and maybe it even sounds cliché to you by now, but your thoughts absolutely determine your actions. When you have a negative thought life you have all but crushed your own dreams before you've even started pursuing them. Telling yourself, "I'm going to fail," or "I'm stupid for even having this dream," or "I'm always going to be the way I am right now," is a self-fulfilling prophecy with severe consequences. I've known amazing men and women who moved from one city or state to another in part to escape the truly negative people and surroundings that were pulling them down, only to have the exact same problems in the new city that they had in the old one because of their thought lives and negative internal dialogues. When your greatest enemies are internal, moving rarely makes even a small difference.

During the period of American slavery, Africans in America were brutalized and demoralized in unthinkable ways—both physical and psychological. It was in that environment that they often embraced a Christian theology of liberation that told them God loved them and had a place for them that was better than what they were experiencing. Similarly, during my lowest moments in life, when my faith really faltered, I tried to hold on to the simple truth that God had a master plan for me that was bigger and higher than the valleys I found myself in.

Even before I was a Christian, my dear mother had convinced me I was somebody special. Every day she would not only tell me how much she loved me but encourage me to dream about whatever it was I wanted to be in the future. After I was assaulted so badly during my sophomore year of high school and missed the next year and a half of school, I was diagnosed with PTSD and had to have counseling to help get me over the hump. As low as I got emotionally, I always felt that if I could survive until I got out of high school, I'd make something of myself. In essence, the very healthy thoughts I had were able to outshine all the negativity I had experienced.

If you are going to have success and build momentum in the next few months, you will need to at least be on the path to having a healthy thought life in which you have a lexicon of positive affirmations to repeat about your own future. I'm not saying you have to stare at yourself in the mirror like Stuart Smalley from *Saturday Night Live* and tell yourself, "I'm good enough, I'm smart enough, and, doggone it, people like me," but even that's better than constantly predicting your own demise. At least start out by leaning toward the belief that you are going to succeed and accomplish your goals.

DROPPING EMOTIONAL BAGGAGE

Between my work as a counselor for incarcerated teenagers and as a pastor in inner-city Atlanta, I've worked with enough people to know that the emotional baggage you carry can and will weigh you down every chance it gets. I want you to know that I mean no disrespect by calling the very legitimate issues of your past "baggage," but I think the metaphor is appropriate. Most of the people who have done you wrong in life have completely moved on. They may not even remember what they did to you, and they certainly don't waste any time thinking about it. What may have been absolutely devastating to you could have been just a quick blip on the radar of their lives. That reality can sting, and if it helps you at all, know that I've experienced this myself. So, while the people who hurt you have moved on, you carry the heavy weight, like an enormous piece of broken-wheeled luggage, around with you everywhere you go. Instead of being free to move and grow and be, you are encumbered with the burden of your emotional past.

But if you are going to where you've never gone before, you will have to leave your emotional baggage behind. Think of it literally as a piece of luggage that is not allowed on the trip you are about to take. Either you take the trip without it, or you stay behind and hold it. Those are your options.

This may mean that you have to actively forgive those who wronged you, or maybe it means you need to get professional counseling to work through it. Or maybe it means you should write down all of the internal things holding you back on a piece of paper and burn it, or all three of those ideas, but you must make it a priority to overcome it.

For me, as a Christian, I literally have to remind myself that if Jesus could freely forgive the men who betrayed him and sent him to die a painful death, then I have no reason why I can't forgive those who have wronged me for much lesser offenses. Throughout my years as a spiritual counselor and guide to people facing emotional pain, I regularly found it gave great solace to have an example like Jesus who found a way to forgive others even if they weren't seeking it.

INNER STRENGTH

While physical strength is the popular subject of infomercials, your inner strength is absolutely essential on this journey. Having a heart and mind free of conflict and strife and an inner life guided by peace, meditation, reflection, learning, grace, and prayer will not only cause doors to open for you and people to want to be around you, it will give you the strength you need to endure moments of struggle and lack. In fact, if every other area of your life fell apart except for this one, you could wait out the hard times with your head held high. Please do not underestimate the impact of this category.

LIFE-GOAL TEMPLATE

✓ Spiritual and Emotional YORG

✓ Two goals you can complete within two months. They should be close to free and be at least loosely related to your YORG.

✓ Three goals you can complete within one year. They should increase in commitment and cost, and some should be related to your YORG.

✓ Five goals that will take one to five years each. They should increase in commitment and cost, and some should be related to your YORG.

✓ Two goals that will absolutely take more than five years to achieve. These are almost YORGs. One should be related to your YORG.

Travel is fatal to prejudice, bigotry, and narrow-mindedness, and

many of our people need it sorely on these accounts.

Broad, wholesome, charitable views of men and

things cannot be acquired by vegetating

in one little corner of the earth all one's lifetime.

—MARK TWAIN

The world is a book and those who do

not travel read only one page.

—AUGUSTINE OF HIPPO

Travel brings power and love back into your life.

—RUMI

Do not follow where the path may lead.

Go instead where there is no path and leave a trail.

—RALPH WALDO EMERSON

13

TRAVEL GOALS

*How Can I Grow by Experiencing the
Beauty and People of the World?*

I had to fight a few people to get this chapter included in the book. Since they didn't get it, I'm going to work extra hard to break it down for you. Trust me; it will be worth it. I'm not knocking anybody, but these goals are probably the most underestimated of them all. The thing is, unless you have done some serious, deliberate traveling outside your comfort zone, you wouldn't really understand the impact it can have on your life. In fact, no category will cause you to learn, stretch, and grow more than this one.

As you know, growing up, I didn't travel much outside of our tiny rural town in Kentucky. I didn't have to. The few little trips my single mom could afford to take us on were all I needed. The road trips we took to Cincinnati, Chicago, Milwaukee, Nashville, and Atlanta exposed me to a brave new world outside of Versailles, Kentucky, and soon became the object of my imagination. As far back as I can remember, I told my mother I was going to move to one of those big cities one day. When my world fell apart as a high school student after I was assaulted, all I could think about was getting well so I could get accepted into Morehouse College and move to Atlanta. Just the reality of knowing that a bigger, better place was out there for me to experience motivated me not only to recover from three spinal surgeries, but to graduate high school on time. In the end, Atlanta exposed me to people and opportunities that simply weren't available to me in my hometown, and moving there was the best decision of my young life.

The interesting thing is, soon after I moved to Atlanta, I met kids and families who had only lived in Atlanta their whole lives and who found it to be a bit of hell on earth for them, even while simultaneously being a dream come true for me. Just as Versailles had become a prison for me, Atlanta had become one for them. Hilariously, in every city I've ever moved to, I've met people who couldn't wait to move out and were stumped as to why I wanted to be there. While New York City and Cape Town, South Africa, represented new adventures for my family, they represented a painful past for those who felt trapped there.

You've heard me say that people can take their bad habits with them wherever they go, and this is definitely true. However, I'm also a big proponent of relocating to a new city if you've truly hit a wall where you are now. The moment you limit yourself to having to find success or a personal breakthrough in your hometown alone, you are immediately making the pool of possibilities incredibly tiny. Often, making a radical move to a new city or country can be just the fresh start you need to get momentum in your life.

UNDERSTAND

In early September of 2001, just a week before 9/11, I was scheduled to travel to South Africa to cover the United Nations World Conference Against Racism for my college newspaper. I had never traveled outside the country and didn't even have my passport at the time, but I couldn't pass up an all-expenses-paid trip to the other side of the world, so I did all I could to make it happen. Had I not made that trip, I am confident my entire life would have played out differently.

While attending that conference in South Africa, I saw and heard men up close and in person who were notorious in my own country: Fidel Castro, Yasser Arafat, and Muammar Gaddhafi. They spoke passionately about what mattered most to them, and while I didn't necessarily identify with what they said, it was a powerful thing just to see these men less as media symbols and more as living, breathing, flawed human beings. Not sound bites, not caricatures, not scapegoats, but just dudes. Seeing them face-to-face impacted me deeply. Good or evil, just or corrupt, whatever they were, from that point forward for me they were real in a way that a thirty-second news segment could never make them.

Later on during my trip, I shook hands with a man who said he was literally "untouchable" in his country. I just happened to sit next to him in a public computer lab. I always like to introduce myself to the people I sit next to. It's one of my strange quirks. It doesn't matter if I'm in a movie theater or crowded restaurant, I'll take a few seconds to shake hands and introduce myself to my new neighbor. When I asked the gentleman at the computer where he was from, he began telling me how his people were badly mistreated and shunned and oppressed in India. I was stunned. To me, he was just a regular old Indian dude, no better or worse than any other Indian I had ever met, but in his own country, as a Dalit, he was treated as less than human. There, it would be seen as "unclean" to shake hands or share a meal with such a man. More than any story I had ever read about American segregation or even apartheid in South Africa, talking to a man who said he would, in a few days, travel back to his homeland, where he would return to being mistreated, broke my heart and made the needless suffering in the world real to me in a way that only meeting such a man could do.

This newfound awareness was further clarified when I saw a naked orphan boy, maybe three or four years old, walking the streets alone. I was crushed. Like any good American, I had witnessed infomercial poverty on late-night television, but this was real. I couldn't change the channel. This boy was on his own, and nobody seemed to care. As I walked up, I tried, ignorantly, to ask him where his family was in English. He had no idea what I was saying and just looked at me with a blank stare. Soon, a security guard from a building we were near came to tell me that this boy, likely an AIDS orphan, was a common sight and that I really couldn't do anything to help. He insisted I keep on walking. I gave the boy some money and, feeling like a coward, went back to my hotel room and cried uncontrollably at the state of that poor boy and the inadequacy of the support I had given him. I pledged from that point forward to always do what I could to help kids in need.

Traveling the world will teach you how to understand the problems of the world in a way that you can't from a short clip on the evening news. Witnessing those problems will help you come to see the problems of your own country more clearly when you notice common sources of issues like racism, poverty, and corruption ten thousand miles apart. It also gives you hope that you can make a difference in ways that seeing photos, videos, or articles online doesn't. In a one-week trip, my world had been rocked. While it may be the case that most people don't want their worlds rocked or don't want to better understand and experience the pain of the poor, for me it did something immeasurable. It showed me, in no uncertain terms, how much I had to be grateful for and how big an impact I could make on the world if I chose to do so.

BECOME A CITIZEN OF THE WORLD

Traveling not only from state to state but from country to country has led my entire family to build an international network of friends. My kids, even the young ones like Ezekiel and Savannah, have had conversations and said prayers and played games with peers in South Africa, Paris, London, Brooklyn, Los Angeles, Kentucky, Atlanta, and beyond. It has given them a confidence in their own skin wherever they go in the world. All of us have learned how to feel at home almost instantly, no matter where we are, and knowing that we've made friends and partners all over the earth causes us to feel like world citizens. When we turn on the news or watch the World Cup or pick up a history book, it's now very likely we will hear or see or read about a place we've already experienced for ourselves.

SEE THE BEAUTY

Since that first trip I made to South Africa as a college student, despite constantly being on a shoestring budget, I've made a concerted effort to allow my life to be enriched by the beauty of the world. Standing on the edge of the Grand Canyon made the earth, now so full of wires and gadgets, feel like an ancient place with history we can only guess at. Looking up at the General Sherman Tree in Sequoia National Park, the largest living tree in the world, had a deep way of centering me that I cannot explain. It had been there since before Jesus was born and was going to be there long after I died.

Seeing all the beauty the world has to offer has caused me to have a deeper belief in and love for God. I've seen things that are so marvelous and spectacular and complicated and breathtaking that I can only conclude they are too awesome to all be miraculous accidents. Even if I didn't believe what I believe, the deep, abiding admiration for the earth that I've been left with would still make me want to preserve and care for it in a way that mowing my backyard or watching a television special on the planet never could.

STRETCH

With every trip that my family and I take to a country we've never visited or a national park we've never camped in, it only increases our desire to see and do more. Our recent trips to Cape Town, Paris, and London didn't make us want to cross those cities off our list, but instead made us want to visit each of them many more times to experience them over and over again.

Sadly, travel, for the sake of your own growth and edification, is something that you won't know you love and actually need until you step out there and do it. My insistence on including it here comes from the reality that my richest experiences, deepest memories, and most profound observations in life came not while I was hanging out in my living room, but when I was experiencing the beauty of the world and her people. What I learned in Haiti about compassion, what I learned in South Africa about determination, what I learned in Paris about beauty, what I learned in London about diversity could not have been learned from textbooks or travel apps. I had to see and smell and touch the places for myself.

World travel will stretch your mind and your beliefs about what's possible. I can't overstate how important this is for anybody developing audacious life goals. I am traveling as I write this book and earlier today, I saw, with my own eyes, a 4,000-year-old Egyptian sphinx at the Louvre museum in Paris, France. It is the largest outside Egypt. Not only was I baffled as to how something so magnificent was built without power tools in the middle of a desert, I was doubly stumped at how it was secured and taken to Paris 200 years ago, before automobiles or jets were even in use. My being stumped had no bearing on the reality, though. What I saw was real, and the sheer feat of its construction and eventual intercontinental travel made me realize that the world has always been full of men and women who look at impossible odds and resolve to figure out how to beat them instead of being beaten by them.

In your small bubble, at your job, in your family, in your neighborhood, it may be almost impossible to witness such history, but travel has a way of making you believe that anything's possible.

World travel will stretch your mind and your beliefs about what's possible.

In fact, when I stood outside Nelson Mandela's jail cell on Robben Island, or looked out over Paris from atop the Eiffel Tower, or looked at the Bible Dr. Martin Luther King had in his pocket when he was assassinated, I couldn't help but wonder if I needed to increase the outrageousness of my life goals. Travel is not a luxury but should be seen as fuel for your journey and pursued every free chance you get. Even if it's increasingly long road trips or staycations close to home where you take full advantage of the culture near you, I demand that you push your travel limits to the extreme!

LIFE-GOAL TEMPLATE

✓ Travel YORG

✓ Two goals you can complete within two months. They should be close to free and be at least loosely related to your YORG.

✓ Three goals you can complete within one year. They should increase in commitment and cost, and some should be related to your YORG.

✓ Five goals that will take one to five years each. They should increase in commitment and cost, and some should be related to your YORG.

✓ Two goals that will absolutely take more than five years to achieve. These are almost YORGs. One should be related to your YORG.

Friendship is always a sweet responsibility,

never an opportunity.

—KHALIL GIBRAN

I would rather walk with a friend in the dark

than walk alone in the light.

—HELEN KELLER

Friendship is the hardest thing in the world to explain. It's not

something you learn in school. But if you haven't learned the

meaning of friendship, you really haven't learned anything.

—MUHAMMAD ALI

When everything goes to hell, the people who stand by you

without flinching—they are your family.

—JIM BUTCHER

14

FRIENDS AND FAMILY GOALS

How Can I Make Sure the People Around Me Know How Much I Love Them?

I live in my head. I've been told this for about a decade by my wife, mother, and brother and even a few friends and colleagues. I don't mean to be this way, but I have found that the people I love the most, while they may hear it from me fairly often, don't always feel like my words match up with my actions. While I want my family and friends to know how deep and real my love is for them, I'm afraid they'd likely describe me as incredibly busy before they would incredibly loving. It stings and embarrasses me a little to even write these words. I think a combination of being a workaholic and having a few extremely high-stress public crises have caused me to become more isolated than I ever imagined I would be. Because I often work from home and travel a lot with my family, I used to think my physical presence or proximity meant I was a good dad or husband, but I've learned the hard way

Nothing touches someone more than when you believe in them at the point at which they want and need it the most.

that physical proximity and emotional nearness are not the same thing.

Of all the goals I want to accomplish by the end of my life, the friends and family goals are easily some of the most important. Simply put, I don't want the people who care for me the most to ever wonder how much I love them. They've been rock-solid reliable for me, and I want to go the extra mile for them and show them, not just with words but with my actions, that I am there for them, too.

As I reflect back over my adult life, it's increasingly clear to me that I have not been an easy man to be married to, or to parent, or to be a sibling of, or even to be a child of. I've had death threats and bodyguards. I've started businesses and lost them. I've been on the news for good deeds and controversy. I've had car accidents and scary ER visits. While being close to me may mean never getting bored, it has also meant riding a never-ending roller coaster. I think I've finally worn myself down enough now to proceed at a normal pace of life, but I want to be absolutely sure that I do my best to make up for lost time with those who've stuck by my side. I want to set new trends for how to show love to my inner circle.

Here are five ways we can show our friends and family we love them. Out of these, we could conceivably create hundreds of unique goals that make sense in each of our own contexts.

1. Give Them a Head Start in Life

The idea of giving the people close to you a head start in life can apply to virtually any situation a family member is facing. Whenever someone you love expresses that they are about to embark on something new, you can choose to respond proactively with something meatier and more meaningful than simply saying, "Good luck." If you live in Manhattan and your friend tells you they are going to audition for a role in a play, offer to pay for them to take a super-nice Uber car there and back. If a teenage family member is a few months away from getting a driver's license, instead of talking to everybody about how scared to death you are about this prospect, offer to pay for a defensive driver's course or take them out on the road yourself. If a young child in your family, or even an adult for that matter, has expressed a love for dance or baseball or cooking or acting or photography, offer to pay for an expert lesson or a series of more affordable lessons to show how much you care. When a family member or friend expresses to you that they are going to college, offer to pay for the application fee or for the required standardized test, or even for a test prep class for that standardized test, and see how much it encourages them. It doesn't matter if they are the type of person who needs the help; your offering will give them the extra push they need to go after it. When someone close to you tells you they have a dream of starting a particular business, call their bluff on it then and there, and tell them you want to pay for the incorporation fees, but only if they incorporate in the next month. Instead of giving them a high five or telling them to go for it (which you should do just on principle), go the extra step, and help them get it launched for real. Nothing touches someone more than when you believe in them at the point at which they want and need it the most.

2. Express It in Words

Life is way too short to assume the people you love know how you feel about them. Maybe you made a mistake in your past, and you're pretty sure everything is smoothed over between you and the person whose feelings you hurt . . . but are you sure? Simply going to your friends and family and letting them know, however old the incidents were, that you are sorry for the mistakes you made will not only free you up emotionally and give you peace, but it will almost always be well received by your loved ones. You don't have to make a big deal out of it, but give it a shot.

Recently, my wife and I both lost our grandmothers. They were anchors in our family. We each have a lot of peace because they knew how much we loved them, but I think Rai and I both wish we had made it just a little bit more abundantly clear. Take time to learn from each elderly member of your family, and have them tell you about your family history. Thank your parents or guardians for all the extra effort they put into loving and raising you.

I grew up in a house where my mother and I told each other "I love you" several times a day. We meant it each time, but we expressed it regularly. I'm that way now with my kids and especially with my wife. What I didn't expect was that my saying it so often makes it mean a little less to her. Instead of just telling her I love her, it means more if I tell her *what* I love about her, or what I love about what she's wearing, or how thankful I am for something particular she worked hard on. She just wants (and deserves) to be noticed, and the truth is that this is pretty much true for each and every one of us.

3. Give Gifts

Who doesn't love a random gift? Even if it's ever so small, a gift given for no reason at all makes even a hard-hearted person feel special. I've learned that a bouquet of flowers on a random Tuesday morning means ten times more to my wife than an even nicer bouquet on Valentine's Day. This same principle is true for every friend and family member you have. My wife is the best at remembering to pick up special little gifts for people from all of the places we visit in the world. It's one of the things I love about her, and she is instilling this same ethic in our kids.

As you think about the longer-term goals, consider giving the people you love shockingly special gifts for the bigger moments in their lives. Buy a family member an item or experience that will get them closer to accomplishing one of their life goals. Pay for them to have a massage or a makeover. Instead of buying yourself a new gadget, buy a new laptop for someone in your family who needs it more than you do. Allow your imagination to run wild, and plan on giving away a few shocking gifts in your lifetime. You'll get just as much pleasure from giving as your friends and family will from receiving.

4. Share Experiences

Rai and I love to create shared memories with one another and with our kids. From our travel around the world to our many visits to American national parks, we believe that creating experiences with our family is worth way more than almost anything else we can do for them, and it doesn't have to cost a lot of money. My son and I love to go to Dodgers baseball games together, and they have seats that are as cheap as ten dollars sometimes. It's just being out with him alone, cheering for a team we love, that matters. My wife takes our girls out to get their nails done together. It's an affordable outing, and they love having some girl time alone. I've also seen her do the same thing with her mother. Even making the effort to learn what your friends and family love and want to do in life is a terrifically warm and loving action done far too infrequently in our world. Do it! Learn the dreams of those you love, and make it your mission to at least loosen the lid on the jar for the life goals of those in your inner circle.

Begin thinking even bigger for your long-term goals, like taking your best friend to five Super Bowls, or going on a trip around the world with your best friends, or visiting every Disney park in the world with the kids. By making the goals bigger than a one-time event or moment that can be too easily delayed, you dramatically increase the likelihood that you will at least get started! For instance, my kids love Disneyland and Disney World. It may take us twenty years, but I'm determined that we will visit every Disney park around the world together. The key is to create adventures and experiences with your loved ones that make sense in your own context and to start planning and positioning yourself for them now. Embrace the unique culture and preferences of your family and go for it!

5. Leave a Legacy

Finally—and this is key—it's important that you consider the type of legacy that you want to leave behind for your friends and family. I'm open to the reality that money and legacy aren't everything and are too often considered one and the same. It is appropriate, though, to make sure that you leave your family well taken care of financially if something should happen to you. Because I'm married with four kids, I've followed Clark Howard's advice and have an insurance plan that is ten times my annual income. This will not only allow my family to take care of any death-related expenses, but will provide a smooth transition after I pass away. For you, this may mean creating a well-written will or leaving a trust behind for charities or colleges that matter to you.

The thing to remember is that legacy is far more than money. My wife now regularly writes e-mails that she saves for each of our kids. She writes them as thoughts come to her that she wants to share with them in case anything ever happens to her and has them saved in her e-mail inbox. Mainly because I don't enjoy crying for hours on end, I have chosen not to read them myself and hope I never have to, but it's one of the most thoughtful things a mother could ever do. Rai and I are also working diligently to leave a legacy of values for our children. We involve them in all our efforts to serve people through humanitarian causes to the point that they'd be disappointed if we didn't. My kids have given me input and support for every business I've ever started, and I am hopeful that I will be leaving them with an entrepreneurial legacy that they will take with them well into adulthood. Whatever this means for you, be sure to include at least one legacy goal in your friends and family goals.

NO REGRETS

While creating goals that directly involve your friends and family may come easily for some of you, I'm fully aware that it may be an extremely touchy subject for others. My intent here is not to force you into contrived moments with people you don't like or have outstanding issues with, but to help you be intentionally outgoing and supportive with the people who matter most to you. A constant regret I hear when someone passes away suddenly is the wish of their family and friends to have been more expressive with their love when they had the time. Go out of your way to be sure that nobody ever has to guess about your love for them. You'll never regret it!

LIFE-GOAL TEMPLATE

✓ Friends and Family YORG

✓ Two goals you can complete within two months. They should be close to free and be at least loosely related to your YORG.

✓ Three goals you can complete within one year. They should increase in commitment and cost, and some should be related to your YORG.

✓ Five goals that will take one to five years each. They should increase in commitment and cost, and some should be related to your YORG.

✓ Two goals that will absolutely take more than five years to achieve. These are almost YORGs. One should be related to your YORG.

The purpose of life is to live it, to taste experience

to the utmost, to reach out eagerly and without

fear for newer and richer experience.

—ELEANOR ROOSEVELT

Nothing ever becomes real 'til it is experienced.

—JOHN KEATS

You've gotta dance like there's nobody watching,

Love like you'll never be hurt,

Sing like there's nobody listening,

And live like it's heaven on earth.

—WILLIAM PURKEY

15

ACCOMPLISHMENT
AND EXPERIENCE GOALS

What Have I Always Dreamed of Doing?

Now that you've determined how you will make your mark in the world, charted a path to good health, gotten yourself on a challenging career track, considered what you must do to stay emotionally well, made plans to travel all over the world, and taken good care of your family and friends, you can finally do some complete randomness for yourself! I honestly think everybody needs some random goals that are completely and totally about them. My thing has always been that without the other well-crafted goals and strategies, not only do these accomplishment and experience goals tend to ring hollow, but they also end up being a bit unrealistic. Without a plan that fully considers every other facet of your life, you will find it very hard—like almost every human being on earth does right now—to actually do something good for yourself.

What I have found to be true time and time again in my own life and in the lives of men and women I really admire is that as you grow and gain momentum in the other six areas of your life, unexpected doors and opportunities open to allow you to finally do things for yourself that you never believed would be possible. It's a perfectly good goal for you to want to purchase a small home on the beach in Southern California, but it's unlikely it will ever happen if you don't hunker down and have real success with your career and finance goals. It's a killer goal for you to have lunch with the president of the United States, but such an event assumes you're either a rock star of generosity, the best at what you do, or fairly wealthy. You get where I'm going with this? I'll never discourage you from having some absolutely insane goals for yourself. Have them and believe in them with your whole heart, but if you want them to be more than pipe dreams, you drastically increase the likelihood they'll happen if you have consistent, measurable growth in the other areas of your life.

In 1999, I was the youngest student government president ever elected at Morehouse College, an all-male HBCU (historically black college or university), and I was having the best time of my life. As a student leader, I was able to hone my skills as a manager, organizer, and motivator, and certainly as a speaker. I worked hard to treat every chance I got to speak before the student body like it might be my last. Every August, before the upperclassmen arrive and classes begin, Morehouse hosts the weeklong New Student Orientation (NSO) for the incoming freshmen. It sounds simple enough, but it's actually a masterfully planned rite-of-passage program unlike anything seen elsewhere in the world. When I entered as a freshman in 1997, NSO had a huge impact on me. After my disastrous high school experience, NSO convinced me that I had an exciting adventure awaiting me at Morehouse.

As the keynote speaker to the freshmen in 1999, I prepared more than I had for any other speech in my life—maybe even to this day. I poured my heart and soul into writing it, rehearsing it, and eventually delivering it with intensity. I've mellowed out a lot since then, but I was an intense dude in those days and I wanted to convey the enormity of the moment that was awaiting these young men. It was probably the best speech I've ever given, and to this day, every few months I meet a guy who was a new student in King Chapel that evening who tells me about the impact it had on his life.

Two days later, I was hiking up the long hill in the center of the campus with friends when three men passed us by. Two looked like new students, and the man in the middle, with a baseball cap pulled low over his forehead, must have been their dad or uncle. I kept on walking like I would have any other time, but suddenly, I had the crazy idea that the man in the middle looked like the Academy Award–winning actor Denzel Washington. He's my favorite actor, and his roles in *Malcolm X* and *Mo' Better Blues* had a big impact on me when I was fighting for my sanity back in Kentucky. I had to turn back and go see if it was him. I ran down the hill, and sure enough, it was Denzel Washington. I motioned for my friends to come back, and we all introduced ourselves.

"Nice to meet you, sir. I'm—"

Laughing with his trademark grin, Denzel looked at me and interrupted, saying, "I know who *the* Shaun King is! We heard you speak in King Chapel. Man, they need to pay you, because all of the parents were hooked after that. Great job. Great job."

We shook hands. I told him how much I admired his work, I introduced myself to his son and another relative, and we went on our way. I could have died with excitement. As soon as he was out of sight, I called Rai—not yet my wife but an incoming first-year student at Spelman College a few hundred yards away—and told her the news. I was excited enough to have met him—that alone was great—but what took it to another level was that he knew my name without my even introducing myself because of something I had done.

At that exact moment, I understood the correlation between hard work in one area of your life and your seemingly unrelated dreams coming true in another. I couldn't have planned it out that way if I wanted to. While fate or luck or coincidence had me out walking that afternoon at the same time as one of my heroes, I am reminded of the quote that says, "Luck is a matter of preparation meeting opportunity."

As you work your plan, over and over again you are going to see the magic that happens when preparation meets opportunity, and I can't wait to hear all about it! Now let me help you think through four areas where you can make some personal goals about what you'd love to either accomplish or experience.

Skills You'd Love to Have

While the development of some skills may fit best in your career and finance goals, or even in your health and fitness goals, this category is the perfect place for the skills you want to develop that don't quite fit in anywhere else. Maybe you want to learn how to become a DJ, or to be a skilled photographer, or you want to learn self-defense, or maybe you want to take a series of advanced cooking classes—all just for your own benefit. Whatever the skill is that you'd love to have, if it doesn't have a neat fit in any other category, this is absolutely the place for it. Like all other life goals, plan on some skills being quick and easy to develop, but leave room for a few that may take years to fully hone.

For instance, maybe you want to have the experience of designing and building your own home. Depending on the cost and how involved you hope to be, this is a goal that it may take you years to achieve. My wife has an awesome goal to be one of the guest hosts on her favorite radio show, *This American Life*. We've just now started to consider what it would take to do such a thing, but it will likely take at least a few years.

Items You'd Love to Own or Collect

As a kid I loved to collect baseball cards. I had over 100,000 cards that I accumulated, and many of them were actually quite valuable. I took meticulous care of them and spent every dime I had from my youth building up my collection. As a newly married twenty-one-year-old experiencing tough times, I had to sell the entire collection to pay our rent one month. It was devastating, but I had to do what I had to do! Now that my son loves sports, I've taught him about collecting cards. I'm also living out my childhood fantasies with him a bit, but I'd love for him and me to purchase some old classic cards or memorabilia together. For his last birthday I bought him some really amazing Jackie Robinson cards, because he'd loved the movie 42 so much.

Maybe you collect cards or trains or Barbie dolls or art and would love to take your collection to another level. Maybe it's not something that is collectible, but you have always wanted to own a vacation home or a certain type of car. As long as it's within reason and doesn't interfere with the rest of your goals, put all these types of goals in this category.

People You'd Love to Meet

If you have people you'd love to meet in life, it's much more likely to happen if you make a goal out of it. Our daughter Kendi is a *huge* fan of the author Ridley Pearson. Because we knew that she'd love to meet him, we kept our eyes open for opportunities. When she finally met him at a Disney expo last year, it was such a big deal for her. He gave her some very sage advice that I think she'll remember for the rest of her life.

> Doing what brings you joy will help you replenish and refuel your own tank so you're able to more effectively serve and lift up others.

Whether it's a person you want to learn from in a workshop or class or just a superstar whom you want to take a selfie with, put that down here.

Events You'd Love to Attend

My entire family and I have so many live television shows that are filmed back home in Southern California that we keep on saying we are going to attend, like a live finale episode of *Survivor*. They all want me to take a shot at being a cast member on *Survivor*, and I'm thinking about adding it to my 100 life goals in this category. Because my family and I are talking about this as a possible goal of mine, my son hilariously now thinks it gives him full permission to tell me how I'm not in good enough shape to be a cast member.

If you want to attend a particular concert or live event like the Super Bowl or game seven of the NBA Finals, this is the place to list those goals. Give yourself the best seats, too! The key here is not to put a limit on what's possible. For instance, I'd like to speak to the senior staff at Twitter, a technology company I love, about setting and pursuing 100 life goals. A lot will have to happen before I'm ever contracted out for such a great opportunity, but by articulating it, I set my life in motion for it to happen. If it's highly unlikely that Twitter will ever ask me to do such a thing now, my odds are at least a bit better than if they didn't even know I cared about such a thing.

PUSH PAST THE GUILT

I won't get into the complex history of why so many of us feel guilty about doing anything good for ourselves, but you must push past this sentiment. It's a problem for me, honestly. In my aim for some semblance of personal humility and compassion for the world, I never want to act like I deserve anything for myself. However, I've long since learned that completely ignoring my own personal joy and fulfillment, while well-intentioned, is shortsighted. Doing what brings you joy will help you replenish and refuel your own tank so you're able to more effectively serve and lift up others.

LIFE-GOAL TEMPLATE

✓ Accomplishment and Experience YORG

✓ Two goals you can complete within two months. They should be close to free and be at least loosely related to your YORG.

✓ Three goals you can complete within one year. They should increase in commitment and cost, and some should be related to your YORG.

✓ Five goals that will take one to five years each. They should increase in commitment and cost, and some should be related to your YORG.

✓ Two goals that will absolutely take more than five years to achieve. These are almost YORGs. One should be related to your YORG.

PART D

HOW TO SEAL THE DEAL

Making Your 100 Life Goals Stick

To finish the moment, to find the journey's end in every step of the road, to live the greatest number of good hours, is wisdom.

—RALPH WALDO EMERSON

A truly good book teaches me better than to read it. I must soon lay it down, and commence living on its hint. What I began by reading, I must finish by acting.

—HENRY DAVID THOREAU

Whatever it takes to finish things, finish. You will learn more from a glorious failure than you ever will from something you never finished.

—NEIL GAIMAN

You cannot expect victory and plan for defeat.

—JOEL OSTEEN

If you are reading these words, I am assuming you've crafted your 100 life goals! If not, stop now and get to work, okay? It may take you a few days or even a few weeks to pull your plan together, but it's essential that you get them done before moving ahead. This is the type of book that you work through and experience.

If you've made it this far and have put together your seven YORGs and a dozen or so unique goals in all seven of the interlocking life-goal categories, I want you to know how amazingly proud of you I am! Woohoo! By taking the time to craft a strategic plan for your life, you have done what 99 percent of the world hasn't. Your life now has a clear sense of direction and purpose. You've built a balanced plan that honors your past while optimistically embracing your future. This time next year you are going to be a brand-new person! The effort you've put into this process will absolutely pay off and now must be matched by an even greater effort to put your awesome plan into action. I can't say it enough, though—I am very, very proud of you.

As soon as you can, tweet me (@ShaunKing) and let me know that you finished crafting your #100LifeGoals (type it just like that), and I'll retweet your tweet and share it with the world—including all the other people who are on this journey with you and are going to be so inspired by the good news! I can't wait to hear from you. If you ever want to share more good news about your journey, be sure to go to 100LifeGoals.com to tell your story.

Now that I've given you the high fives and hugs you deserve, I want to help you seal the deal and make your 100 life goals stick. Too often, when reality hits you in the face, the first things to get thrown away are your dreams and goals. As a man who has had reality smack him in the face more times than he can count across the years, I get it. It's very easy to simply go back to the old way of doing things. Dreams die far too easily in our world. In the final chapters of this book, I'm going to teach you how to keep your plan close, surround yourself with the right coaches and teammates, and overcome the inevitable adversity we are all sure to face at one time or another. I believe in you and in your potential to make your plan a reality, but what it takes to get a good thing started is not what it takes to keep it going. As a serial starter, this has been a very difficult lesson for me to learn.

You have to ask yourself this question: would I rather be an awesome starter who rarely finishes the race or a slow starter who always finds my way across the finish line? Maybe you've been a great starter in the past, but now it's time for you to give every-thing you've got to being not just an architect but a master builder.

You've set a strong foundation, but now it's time for you to finish the job. Just know that this won't be a onetime thing but that you will constantly find yourself needing to make adjustments and improvements to your plans and to the many exciting actions you will soon begin taking.

Coming together is a beginning. Keeping together is progress.
Working together is success.

—HENRY FORD

It is literally true that you can succeed best and quickest by
helping others to succeed.

—NAPOLEON HILL

A boat doesn't go forward if each one is rowing their own way.

—SWAHILI PROVERB

A person standing alone can be attacked and defeated, but two
can stand back-to-back and conquer. Three are even better, for
a triple-braided cord is not easily broken.

—ECCLESIASTES 4:12 (NLT)

16

TEAMWORK MAKES YOUR DREAMS WORK

Coaches and Teammates

Pop culture loves to exclude teamwork from the stories it tells about successful individuals. Without fail, time and time again, undoubtedly talented men and women who were surrounded by a stellar team of unnamed colleagues and comrades are lifted up and celebrated as if they accomplished everything on their own. Individuals get the credit that teams deserve. The story of one lone, villainous man who ruined a country or the one valiant hero who saved it is both fictional and overtold. I love those stories as much as the next person, but they just aren't true. For many reasons, the narrative of one person who had a brilliant idea and turned it into a world-changing business is just easier on the ears and the mind. Part of us wants it to be the case that somebody can be sitting around, get inspired, and then save the world all by themselves. This is pretty much the hero narrative of Batman, Iron

Man, Spider-Man, Superman, Captain America, and every other comic book superhero ever created, but when we impose it on real people or even adopt it as the method we plan on using in life, we set ourselves up for failure.

Steve Jobs, outside of the tech world, is heralded as the founder of Apple, but he had an indispensable cofounder in Steve "Woz." Wozniak. Having completely designed, programmed, and built the Apple I and Apple II computers by himself, Woz is responsible for securing the early foundation of Apple. In fact, the Apple II was the very first personal computer ever able to display color graphics and became one of the first highly successful mass-produced personal computers. Even after Woz left Apple, he invented and produced the first universal remote control that was brought to market. Though he is a brilliant man, we rarely hear about Woz because of a larger-than-life comeback that Steve Jobs helped stage for Apple nearly twenty years after they founded the company together. I'm a huge fan of Steve Jobs, but even after he helped Apple become the iconic tech company it is today, he was surrounded by some of the most talented designers and programmers in the world. Of course, Jobs was both the glue and the driving force behind the company we know and love, but the true success of Apple must be attributed to its stellar team.

If the Steve Jobs illustration works, then the Dr. Martin Luther King illustration is even better. No modern leader had a better spouse, extended family, and support network with coaches, advisers, mentors, editors, assistants, and students than Dr. King. Talented, brave, and brilliant, Dr. King was a man made for his time, but he was effective not only because he had a real support system, but because the entire civil rights movement had its own complex set of leaders, fund-raisers, and organizers in at least 100 American cities that had virtually nothing to do with Dr. King. Even the "I Have a Dream" speech itself, while creatively and powerfully delivered by Dr. King alone, had skilled editors looking over every single line before it was delivered. None of this is said to minimize Dr. King (never that) but to shine a light on the reality that Dr. King was as successful as he was because of the robust network of skilled support he leaned on.

The list of men and women hailed as lone heroes and icons who actually had essential support teams behind and beside them is not a short one. In our clamor for messianic heroes in business, culture, and politics, we not only do their full stories a disservice when we omit the narrative of the essential support team, but we ultimately do ourselves an even bigger disservice by striking out to pursue our dreams alone because we thought people like Steve Jobs and Dr. King did so, too. When you look in virtually any field and see someone who is highly successful, be it Michael Jordan and Kobe Bryant in basketball, or Jay Z and Kanye in hip-hop, or Spielberg and Eastwood in film direction, each and every one of them has a real supporting cast of teammates, advisers, coaches, and experts who take what they do and make it better. In fact, the more successful someone is, the more likely it is that they actually have an incredibly long list of supporters behind the scenes who labor to make what they do possible.

As you strike out to pursue your 100 life goals, I cannot overstate the importance of proactively building your team. At first, your team may just be an online life-goals support group or one friend or family member who always has your back. That's okay. I just need you to understand that the longer you stand alone in this pursuit, the more likely it is that you will hit a wall, get burned out, be discouraged, or get stumped by a problem. Even worse, it is exponentially more likely that you will quit early if you try to be a lone ranger with this endeavor.

No external factor increases the likelihood of your success more than surrounding yourself with a strong team. Period.

I would love to relive some of the opportunities that I've had over the past fifteen years, but this time with the knowledge and appreciation I have now for the value of a team. So determined to do life on my own and to prove myself to the world, I consistently struggled as a leader in the past because of my inability to do life well with others, whether it was my being a fairly introverted person or the fact that I was still

> **No external factor increases the likelihood of your success more than surrounding yourself with a strong team. Period.**

hung up on times when other people had failed me before. I can think of a dozen strong people who offered to be on my team in some shape, form, or fashion over the years, but I was just too bullheaded or broken to accept them. Ultimately, the loss was mine when I ended up struggling mightily in situations where I could have clearly succeeded with even a little help. I don't want to pretend that accepting help is what I'm best at now, because it isn't, but I am drastically better than I used to be and I've seen dramatic results.

WHO ARE YOUR COACHES?

The highest-performing people in the world, ranging from athletes and entertainers to business leaders and charity executives, have coaches and mentors. I didn't know this. They don't teach you that in high school or college, but it's true. The best CEOs and leaders at least have a few informal mentors and advisers whom they go to for guidance or insight, but a significant percentage of them actually have formal coaches, mentors, or trainers that they pay, and pay well, to keep them focused, sharp, healthy, and growing. If you could look right now at your 100 life goals, including your YORGs, and tell me that you can accomplish them all without the training and guidance of any experts, then your goals aren't ambitious enough.

LeBron James, currently the best basketball player in the world and one of the greatest athletes of our time, has nearly a dozen coaches and trainers. None of them are as good as he is at basketball, and I am almost 100 percent sure that none of them are as fit or as strong as he is. When he was in middle school, he was already a better basketball player than 99 percent of people in the world. He's been special for a long time. The thing is, though, LeBron James knows that 400 other players in the NBA want the same thing he wants: an NBA championship. While LeBron may be more gifted and more athletic than all of them, he also knows that in order for him to succeed as a champion, it's going to take coaches who specialize in studying defense, coaches who specialize in studying offense, coaches who specialize in crafting game plans against each of his opponents, trainers who specialize in what he should eat, trainers who specialize in how he should stay fit, and even trainers who advise him on when he should go to bed and how long he should sleep to be a peak performer. His own skills and hard work opened up a lot of doors, but to be a champion and remain a champion, even LeBron James needs a whole slew of coaches.

Can we agree on this? If LeBron James is the best there is in his field and still needs coaching, then you and I do, too.

Coaching Networks

Before I ever formed Life Goals University to coach and guide people through setting and pursuing their life goals, I joined four different coaching networks that changed my professional life. I'm hooked, actually. Before I joined the first one, which people I admire, like Michael Hyatt and Casey Graham, kept raving about, I'll admit that I was skeptical. It cost $2,000 to join, and it was almost all the money I had at that point. The coaching program is called Product Launch Formula and is led by Jeff Walker. It's completely online, and he teaches his students how to create and launch online products. It's intense, but in six weeks I learned more about launching a product than I had in the previous six years. I couldn't get enough of it, and I knew that if I took the steps he advised us to take that I would be able to more than make up for the investment I made.

Second, I joined Experts Academy, led by Brendon Burchard. Brendon was actually an early student of Jeff Walker, and Experts Academy helped me to learn how to diversify my income by doing what I love. It built on the foundation of Product Launch Formula and gave me a clear vision for what my life could look like for years to come. I regularly go back and study what I learned from Brendon, and he is one of the most motivational and educational coaches anybody could ever have.

Then I needed some hands-on guidance to help build Life Goals University so that I could reach and teach people effectively online. Hands-on consulting always costs more than online coaching, but it is specialized just for what you need. I contracted Casey Graham, one of the foremost experts in the world at building online businesses, and his entire team to help me build Life Goals University from the ground up. The coaching I received was the single biggest investment I've ever made for my own future. I could have tried to wing it without any help, which is what I normally do, but I was in over my head with some of the technical aspects of online campaigns and payment systems and needed his help.

Finally, for about $20 a month, I joined my fourth coaching program, called Marketing Genesis, taught by Andy Jenkins and Mike Filsaime. They are experts in creating simple but engaging online videos and campaigns that really impact people. Because I was a beginner in the field of creating videos and campaigns, I felt like I could really use their help, and it has been well worth the investment.

After joining these four coaching programs and having real success, I joined Tribe Writers, led by Jeff Goins, to help me understand how I could really throw myself into becoming a full-time author. Not only did Jeff teach me practical writing strategies that I use almost every single day, but he gave me the confidence to begin seeing myself and introducing myself as an author. While it sounds like a small thing, Jeff helped me flip a switch in my mind that has taken my writing quality and productivity up several notches.

Toward this same end, I joined Platform University, led by Michael Hyatt, for about the same cost. Few people know more about building a platform to reach and teach people than Michael. Quickly, through him, I learned how to best use my existing social networks, e-mail list, and blog to keep people connected and informed. It was well worth it. Six coaching programs in one year may sound ridiculous. Heck, it may actually *be* ridiculous. All I know is that from them I learned how to transition out of the rat race and into what I love doing, and that is no easy feat. The truth is, I'm not sure I could have paid these six coaching programs enough for what I learned and the impact they had on me. Not only have I made back the cost financially, but the freedom I have because of what I learned is priceless.

I want to note that none of these coaches knew I was going to mention them here, and none of them are getting any kickbacks from me. The services they've provided me, and the thousands of other people they coach online, stand on their own merit. After going almost my entire professional life without any coaching, I think I grew and learned more on purpose in the first year I received coaching than I did in all the previous years combined. There is something about using your hard-earned money on coaching that lights a fire under your butt to actually learn the lessons and put them into action. It took me a while to figure this out, but with almost no exceptions, I have found that when I have given someone free access to my paid coaching programs, they rarely finish and are usually the least devoted students I have. It's not that people who don't have money are bad students, but when someone makes coaching a financial priority they are also willing to carve out the time and attention it deserves.

I stand by all of the coaching programs I've named here and obviously stand by Life Goals University, but you have to choose what works well for you. Try to find a program that has at least a short free trial so that you can test it out a bit and see if it's for you. I took some big financial risks with the coaching programs I joined and wouldn't always advise that. Work within your budget and plan, and only take calculated risks when you know you are going to do the work to make it all pay off. With every month that passes, more and more highly specialized coaching programs are formed for every aspect of your life. My hope is that one day you'll be leading one of your own!

Private Coaching

By and large, private coaching is going to cost more than an online coaching network, but sometimes you are going to need a degree of one-on-one attention and must find an executive coach or trainer to help guide you where you need to go. Before you give up on the idea of having a paid private coach because of cost, understand that sometimes you may only need a few short sessions to get you moving in the right direction. The price ranges vary so drastically from field to field and coach to coach, but I can assure you that a quality coach in your field is within reach. I also want you to broaden your mind as you begin to think about who coaches are and what services they provide. You may need any of the following:

- Financial coach/adviser to help you completely overhaul your financial life, including debts, investments, estate planning, and more

- Personal trainer to help craft a customized fitness plan based on a thorough analysis of your strengths, weaknesses, and plan for the future

- Career/business coach to help you navigate the very tricky terrain ahead for your career and business goals

- Spiritual guide/counselor/psychologist to help give you the inner strength, peace, and habits you are bound to need along the way

- Marriage coach/family counselor to help you think and work through what it means to have a strong and healthy family today

- Skills coach to help you grow rapidly in a very specialized field of your choice

Advisory Boards

An increasing number of people, including myself, are creating advisory boards as a form of accountability. In essence, I have asked four people I know, trust, and admire if they would be willing to occasionally offer me advice and guidance as needed. They don't vote or have any veto power in my life, but they are there as a form of support. They don't have to attend any meetings, and we have all agreed that we will connect in person as we have time and are able to do so. I send them regular e-mail updates about how I'm doing, good and bad, and ask for their insights as they see fit. Far from being a board of directors, this group of advocates is there in great part to remind you that you aren't alone in life. While this may seem like advice overkill for some, I find that it helps me to know that I have people who have committed to caring about me on another level. When you first form your personal advisory board, consider three things:

1. The burden for communicating with your advisers is completely and totally on you. You must make this as easy as possible for them.

2. You must be willing to meet with them or speak to them when it works for them.

3. It's a good idea for you to support them and their projects every chance you get.

Social Media

As you likely know, social media is a big deal in my life. Beyond the fact that it has been how I've made a living for the past several years, it has also been how I've met and communicated with so many men and women I admire all over the world. While nothing is a substitute for a coaching network, private coaching, or an advisory board, following the top experts in the world on social media is an amazing way to get a real glimpse into their world. As a rule, I used to follow everybody on Twitter who followed me until I realized that it made it very difficult to hear and learn from the experts I was following. Whereas it may be nearly impossible for you to be directly coached by Oprah Winfrey, she is on Twitter and Instagram sharing life lessons every day. The same is true for the CEO of nearly every company you can imagine, your favorite authors, health gurus, athletes, sports coaches, top motivational speakers, and more.

I also make it a point to follow people who I think are just a few steps ahead of where I am now. It can be amazingly difficult to look at the number one person in your field and understand how they got from where you are now to where they are now, but when you follow people who are currently just a year or two ahead of you, not only can you literally scroll back and see what they were posting back then, but you can chart their progression and see what their journey looked like. Also, by following the experts and leaders you need to learn from, you'll probably discover what they're reading, the conferences they attend, how they are getting better, what's really grabbing their interest, and more. If I had to give up all of the forms of coaching, I'd miss this one the most, because it comes at me from every angle from a diverse set of experts every single day for free. That's hard to beat.

Books

Books, in my opinion, are still one of the best tried-and-true methods for being remotely coached and taught by the top experts in the world. Until I wrote this book, I honestly had no idea how amazingly difficult and time-consuming it is to put 75,000 meaningful words together. I know all books aren't created equal, but if someone you admire has written an autobiography or a guide of some sort, you can rest assured they put the very best lessons and anecdotes they have to offer in there. As simple as it sounds, one of the first steps I always ask my students to take is to send me a list of the ten best books on the topic they need help in. I'm not trying to insult your intelligence, but you can discover what the best books on any given topic are by looking at the bestseller lists from all the top online booksellers, searching Goodreads, and even searching "best books on [fill in the blank]" on Google or your favorite search engine.

Before I ever climbed my first mountain, I read five amazing books on mountaineering. I wanted to familiarize myself with the language, the challenges, and particularly the level of preparation needed to do such a thing before I actually did it. By the time I stepped foot on a mountain for the first time I knew the difference between a crampon and a similar-sounding feminine health product and knew that self-arrest wasn't when you bust yourself for a crime but when you smartly stop yourself from falling down a mountain.

I keep this same habit of devouring the five to ten top books on a topic before I jump into it headfirst with almost everything I do. For less than $100 you can usually purchase the top five books on whatever it is you're trying to learn. The key is to make sure they don't just decorate your shelves (or your e-reader) but that you actually read them and internalize the lessons.

Three newer technologies and one old-school institution have made reading the best books a breeze for me and so many others:

E-BOOKS. On my iPad, I have an e-book reader that I swear by. Tablets are more affordable and powerful than they've ever been and they allow you to carry a large volume of books and resources in a small package. Through my e-reader, I subscribe to four magazines and have a library of over 100 books I've purchased at my disposal. I love paper books as much as the next person, but being able to carry so many books and magazines with me everywhere I go makes this app indispensable for me. Books are normally a few bucks cheaper when you buy them this way, you get them instantly, and you never have to worry about losing them again.

AUDIBLE. I have been a faithful subscriber to Audible for almost a decade. As the leading provider of downloadable audiobooks, Audible has virtually every book imaginable for you to listen to. They also have a feature now that allows you to listen to an audiobook whenever you can, and when you pull out your e-reader later to read that same book, it will open up to wherever you left off in the audiobook, and vice versa. Because I'm on the go a lot—and I'm guessing you are, too—audiobooks allow me to make much better use of my time on the road, on the train, in line, on the plane, or any other place where physically reading a book is a bit more difficult. Or maybe you just don't dig reading very much. If that's the case, Audible might be just what the doctor ordered. And if you choose a book that you don't like very much, they allow you to swap it out for another book at no cost.

OYSTER. Oyster is kind of like the Netflix of books. It's an app for your tablet that allows you, for a small monthly fee, to read as many books as you want. Their selection is getting bigger and bigger every month, and my wife and I are finding that we can always discover something great to read there. At just about ten dollars a month, it's a steal and costs less than buying even one book.

YOUR PUBLIC LIBRARY. As old-school as they are, public libraries still keep their collections up-to-date and allow you to check out your favorite books for free. If you're on a tight budget or if you simply want to use your book-buying budget for something else, take full advantage of your public library. Always consider searching the website first to see if they have what you need, but consider the possibility that they may have great books on the topic that you've never thought of. Sometimes I check out a book at the library first before I decide if I want to buy it as a permanent resource.

WHO ARE YOUR TEAMMATES?

If great coaching helps you know where to go and how to get there, a strong team is the vehicle that is most likely to get you to your destination in one piece. I've said it many times already, but being a team player is a new skill I'm developing. I am a complete work in progress with this, but I am likely the very best witness for what happens when you either fail to cultivate a team or underutilize the one you're lucky to already have. I'm trying to expose this weakness of mine with the hope that many of you who are reading this will find my failings with teamwork strangely familiar and be motivated to push beyond your own weaknesses and grow like I am.

If you are a loner, notoriously shy, fiercely independent, or a full-fledged introvert, I get you. Outside of being with my wife and kids, I could go months at a time without any human interaction and be just fine with it. I don't know why I am this way, but it seems to be getting worse with age. The big reason this is a problem is that most things worth doing in life take a team to accomplish. Even goals that seem like they can be completed with no help at all almost always require a coach or a teacher or a guide of some sort. You may be the driving force behind your goals, whether you want to climb Mount Everest or publish a series of action novels or open up a soul food restaurant, but you won't be able to accomplish even one of them on your own. Humans are symbiotic, interactive beings, and no matter how much we may want to break away from humanity and be on our own sometimes, it just doesn't work that way. We must interact with people and trust them and go on adventures with them if we are going to maximize our full potential. It's nonnegotiable, and the benefits are irreplaceable.

> We must interact with people and trust them and go on adventures with them if we are going to maximize our full potential.

As a part of a team, instead of being forced to learn every lesson and discover every trick on your own, your teammates will share what's working for them (and what's not working). Together, you'll be working with shared momentum as you move in the same direction, with the same sense of purpose, fueled by the same passion for life. Excitement is contagious, and as you see your fellow team members celebrate victories large and small, it will add extra fuel to your fire to push you toward your own goals. It's as close to an unstoppable force as you've ever experienced.

Another benefit is the high expectation you operate under as a part of a team. It's great to be self-motivated, but when you are on a team of people who expect you to give your best day in and day out, your willingness to slack off and do a crap job plummets. Group standards have a way of making sure that your low point never gets too low. This is the primary reason why Alcoholics Anonymous, Celebrate Recovery, and other step-based programs work so well. Each member must do their best work, but when they are struggling they are reminded of how hard the entire group is working to be their very best. Championship teams in sports and successful teams throughout the marketplace thrive in great part because high expectations create the social pressure needed for peak performance. This is also why the fastest sprinters are more likely to set records against other fast opponents versus running alone—the pressure creates speed.

Perhaps the best benefit of being a part of any team, though, is that you get to be around people who have very different strengths and weaknesses from you. This not only gives you the opportunity to grow in your area of weakness, learning from somebody who has that natural strength, but it also gives you the important opportunity to teach others how you do what you do well—which, I think, is the best way to go from good to great in anything. For instance, after nearly ten years of working in the charity world full-time, I was shocked at how much I was able to grow from just two years of full-time work in the tech start-up space. I knew so little about apps and patents and venture capital three years ago, but I am at least proficient in all three worlds now. I grew, because I was on a team made up of people with strengths that were vastly different from mine.

Ultimately, teammates are essential to your growth and success. They can come in various forms, and whatever way you choose to pursue them, I encourage you to do so with seriousness and commitment.

Online Support Teams

I am a huge advocate for online support teams. We provide them through Life Goals University at 100LifeGoals.com, but you can also find or form your own. The miracle of technology allows you to create deep and meaningful connections with people you may never meet in person but find that you have more in common with than anybody in your bloodline or zip code. Before social media, it could take years and years to find someone who shared your narrow interests or particular passions. Online support teams change all that; it doesn't matter if someone lives on a different continent or comes from a radically different culture. Because you share an essential affinity with them, you connect instantly. I've created and led dozens of online support teams and have found the relationships formed from them are just as real as anything that ever happens offline. Give one a try as soon as you can.

Specialty Teams

As you look over your 100 life goals, consider whether you have any goals that would allow you to become a part of a specialty team. For instance, I have a goal of obtaining my black belt in Brazilian jiujitsu. This goal not only requires me to have a coach, but is best obtained by being part of a competitive team. My wife, just as a hobby, has joined an adult tap-dancing team and loves it. My children, Ezekiel, Savannah, Kendi, and Tae, have all been members of various sports teams, dance teams, and plays that required them to form real bonds with their peers and coaches. You may consider becoming a member of a local religious body, an investment group, or a certain trade organization centered around a certain skill, like filmmaking or disaster relief. The more specialty teams you join that are in line with your life goals, the better.

Life-Goal Partners

Don't beat yourself up if you don't have one yet, but if you ever get the chance to partner up with one person offline to pursue your 100 life goals, you've done a good thing. This may be a spouse, your best friend, a sibling, or a coworker, but it should be someone you trust and actually like to be around. If, for some reason, you sincerely don't have that person in your life today, begin forming the type of relationships that would produce such a bond. Although I'm a real online type of guy, the feedback, support, and encouragement I get from my wife and kids make all the difference for me. We all have goals that we pursue together and do everything we can to help each other achieve them. When you find a person like this that you can text, talk with, and hang out with in person, treat them like gold.

Friends and Family

Your friends and family can be a part of your team as well, albeit in their own ways. It's great when they rally around you as you seek to reach your goals, but I want to make one point clear: family and friends can love you without making your dreams their own. I've seen good people fall out with their parents, siblings, and friends because they didn't support their goals the way they imagined they would. Don't do that. Your family and friends have their own goals in life, and you have yours. You cause yourself unnecessary stress when you constantly fall out with family and friends over their per-ceived indifference to your goals. Feel free to let them know ways they *can* support you, but do it with an open hand and heart and zero expectations. This way, every time one of them does, it will be a great surprise and a privilege. Then you can return the favor by supporting them with their own goals.

I only have two exceptions for this rule, but I want you to focus more on how you can live it out than on how you can hold it in front of somebody as a form of judgment.

SUPPORT YOUR KIDS. It's hard for kids to achieve anything on their own without active emotional support and financial underwriting from their parents. If you have kids, I charge you with helping them understand their goals, set them, and pursue them like crazy. It will be an amazing adventure and extremely fulfilling when they achieve even the smallest goal. By instilling this work ethic in your kids at an early age, you are making a smart down payment on their futures.

SUPPORT YOUR SPOUSE. Few things will strengthen the bond between two married people more than selflessly finding ways to help your spouse achieve their goals. Seek out ways to make your spouse's dreams come true every chance you get. Don't use my admonition against your spouse, but use it as a new way for you to express your own love. Of course, the hope is that your spouse will be motivated to return the favor, but don't let this be your only motivation.

SHARING THE BURDENS AND THE VICTORIES

At my core, I'm a loner, but I've learned to appreciate the beauty and benefits of sharing the burdens and the victories of life with those around me. Personal achievement is easily misunderstood to mean how you pursue your goals by yourself. The truth, however, is that the strength of the team you build exponentially increases the likelihood that you will achieve your dreams, and the quality of your team means that you will actually enjoy the pursuit in ways that a solitary life could never match. It can be hard work to build healthy relationships, but I assure you that it's more than worth it in the end.

The most beautiful people we have known are those who have known defeat, known suffering, known struggle, known loss, and have found their way out of the depths. These persons have an appreciation, a sensitivity, and an understanding of life that fills them with compassion, gentleness, and a deep loving concern. Beautiful people do not just happen.

—ELISABETH KÜBLER-ROSS

You may encounter many defeats, but you must not be defeated. In fact, it may be necessary to encounter the defeats, so you can know who you are, what you can rise from, how you can still come out of it.

—MAYA ANGELOU

Nothing in the world is worth having or worth doing unless it means effort, pain, difficulty. . . . I have never in my life envied a human being who led an easy life. I have envied a great many people who led difficult lives and led them well.

—THEODORE ROOSEVELT

17

OVERCOMING ADVERSITY

How to Bounce Back When Life Gets Crazy

Overcoming adversity is probably my greatest area of expertise. I can't say I'm proud to be a bounce-back expert, but it's definitely who I am. I am the Ric "Nature Boy" Flair of bouncing back. If you aren't a fan, he's the famous professional wrestler who won the World Heavyweight Championship belt a record sixteen times—which, by default, also means he lost it a whopping sixteen times.

I thought of this one time when I was watching a boxing match featuring Oscar De La Hoya, and the announcers were bragging about how strong Oscar's chin was. He had only been knocked out once in his career, and that was because of a perfectly timed body shot. The one experienced boxer among them, Roy Jones Jr., said something I never forgot: "Having a good chin is actually code for getting punched a lot." He was right. Oscar got punched a lot and seemed to know how to endure the punishment and push through. Muhammad Ali was the same way. While I'll agree that it's better to never lose your championship or get punched in the face, how we all respond to adversity defines our futures.

If you locked yourself in a room and refused to pursue even one life goal, you still wouldn't be immune to adversity. Sickness, loss, financial woes, emotional ups and downs—they hit all of us at one time or another. Some people are able to stave off hard times better, but Jesus said it like this: "The rain falls on the just and the unjust." Lord knows some people out there have had a harder life than I have, but I've learned through many great trials how to bounce back from situations and circumstances that have taken a lot of people out. If you can overcome the roadblocks, if you can craft your life goals in a way that builds momentum, and if you can get your journey started, the only thing that has the chance to derail you is adversity, and it doesn't have to win. You can prevail over it.

> **How we all respond to adversity defines our futures.**

Lesson #1: Expect Hard Times and Remain Optimistic

A lot of people expect hard times to come, but it leaves them in a place of negative pessimism because they get fixated on all that's likely to go wrong. This is unhealthy. Other people are so optimistic that when hard times come, it hits them like a shocking ton of bricks and ruins their trouble-less view of the world. This isn't ideal either. A happy medium exists between these two ways of seeing the world, and your ability to find it will help you tremendously in life. Having a deep understanding that we live life in seasons—with highs and lows, ups and downs, winter, summer, spring, and fall—is the first step to having a more balanced view of your future. Even more than that, you learn how to prepare better to face the many forms of weather that will come in those seasons.

Physically speaking, I don't know anyone more prepared for every form of weather than my wife. She makes sure all six members of our family have raincoats and rain boots and umbrellas for the wet weather; lightweight jackets for cool nights and autumn days; heavy coats, gloves, and hats for whatever winter weather we may face; and, living in Southern California, she always has whatever we need to do well in the sun, be it sunscreen, spray fans, water bottles, the right clothes, or umbrellas for the beach. She has all of the clothes packed away in labeled containers ready to be brought out at a moment's notice. It's her way, but it also takes great effort. The kids and I are very lucky to have her looking out for us.

Could you imagine, though, what it would be like if Rai, no matter what the forecast or season or current conditions, insisted on preparing us for just one season all year long? I'm imagining being on our way to a summer day at the beach dressed like we're about to build a snowman in Central Park. Or perhaps being constantly dressed like it's raining—umbrellas opened all the way, rain boots and ponchos in full effect—in the middle of a drought. We'd look like modern-day Noahs expecting a flood. All of this sounds preposterous, but when you live your life as if it's always going to be good or always going to be bad, you're pretty much wearing flip-flops, shorts, and a T-shirt in a blizzard.

Instead, always aim to live life with a prepared awareness that both ups and downs are on their way and neither will last forever. Be thankful and treasure every great moment that comes your way in those good seasons. There are few things worse than someone who refuses to enjoy success or happiness because they know it won't last forever. That's like hating chocolate cake because you know that you'll eventually have to take the last bite, or not listening to a beautiful song or watching a stellar movie because you know it'll eventually come to an end. When you find yourself in a bad season, though, don't fall into a deep funk thinking you'll never find your way out of the hole you're in. You will. You always do—one step at a time.

Lesson #2: Squeeze Value out of the Valley

Some of the most essential life lessons can be learned during your lowest moments. In fact, if you find yourself in the same low moment over and over and over again, it's highly likely that you keep ending up there because you refuse to learn the lesson that low moment is trying to teach you. Low moments are like that sometimes. I do understand that when you have hit a wall, it's hard to gather yourself up to ask the wall what it wants to teach you. I get it. You hate the wall. After you get done hating it, though, you must take several deep, calming breaths and consider what lessons you can learn from the state you find yourself in.

Only recently, after hitting a few walls one too many times, have I made the sincere transition into learning from my troubles. I've been pretty doggone good at bouncing back from them, but

I found myself ending up in a similar place a year or two afterward because I didn't take the mature and deliberate opportunity to squeeze value out of my valley moments. Valleys have gotten a bit of a bad rap. The truth is, the higher you climb a mountain, the less life can survive there. Valleys, though, are actually known for their abundantly fertile soil. Rich plant life and streams of water in the valley attract

> The lessons and nourishment you need for the mountaintop are likely found in the valley.

animals from far and wide. We are often so determined, though, to climb to the mountaintop that we fail to get what we need from the valley when we're there.

The mountain and the valley actually rely on each other in the most essential ways, and the lessons and nourishment you need for the mountaintop are likely found in the valley. Yes, you may be far away from your destination, but the valley can be a place to rest and be refreshed if you so choose. If you insist on rushing your way out of your low moments without learning the lessons they want to teach you, you are bound to keep repeating them and rubbing yourself and others raw in the process.

Try asking yourself, "What is this moment trying to teach me?"—or something similar that works well for you—the next time, and every time, you find yourself in the valley. It will allow you to immediately pivot away from a position of self-pity to one of empowerment and focus.

DEALING WITH REAL LIFE

Let's get practical and spend some important time talking about the real-life situations you could find yourself in. I've experienced every one of these challenges, some more than once, and bounced back from them. I've also counseled and coached hundreds of people through them. The key is for you to know that you *can* recover and to always find a way to learn the lessons that come out of those low moments.

When You Are Broke or Struggling Financially

I've been completely broke many times. I'm talking about having zero dollars in my bank account and way more month than money. When Rai and I were newlyweds, we were both still college students back in Atlanta, we had a baby on the way, and we were living off student-loan refunds. The American economy was in shambles, and we were winging it. The only job I could find that would still allow me to attend school full-time was an airport security job. Sweet as could be, Rai would pack me a lunch every day, and I would wear my security uniform (I even had a mesh hat) and head out to work the night shift at the airport. It paid the bills and kept us housed and fed the first year of our marriage. We've had many hard times since then, including having to sell our first home in a hurry, selling everything we owned and moving across the country on a shoestring budget, and cramming all of us into a one-bedroom apartment in New York City for a while.

So if you find yourself broke or struggling, consider these strategies we learned:

1. Work a job (or two or three) that you don't like very much until you can transition into what it is you love. A surefire recipe for disaster is quitting a good job before you are fully ready to make a living from your dream. It's a tricky transition, but I strongly advise you not to quit an income-producing job until you are sure you will have another income in place. I'm also personally against your being unemployed by choice while you look for the perfect job. Companies prefer to hire employed people—even if this means you are working retail or waiting tables. Get a job to pay the bills, and look for a job in your off-hours.

2. Reduce your expenses to the lowest possible amount. Make rent, utilities, food, and transportation your primary budget, and cut out everything else you can technically do without, like cable/satellite, random shopping, eating out, Internet, memberships, etc. Squeeze your budget until it is bone-dry, and refuse to add another dime to it. Do free stuff for fun.

3. Make a budget and pledge to stick with it, even if you only have a few bucks. You are never too broke to abandon budgeting. Tracking every dollar of income and every expense almost always saves you money. In fact, the less money you have, the more important it is that you keep track of every nickel and dime coming in and out.

4. If you have a loving family member or friend who will allow you to live with them for a set period of time while you increase your income, decrease your expenses, and make changes to how you handle money, take full advantage of this opportunity. Make a real contract with them for how long you'll stay and what you will pay when you can. This will give them a great deal of peace and light a fire under you to make some moves. Even consider having a roommate after you get back on your feet to share the load. This is very common in the most expensive cities of the world for good reason.

When You Get Fired

I've been fired before. That was in 2006, and I haven't worked for anyone else since. It sucked. When I lost my job as a resident director at Morehouse College, Rai was pregnant with Ezekiel, we had Kendi and Tae, and we actually lived in a dorm on campus. It may sound like hell, but it was my dream job at the time. Our bills were virtually covered, I received a small salary, and the work wasn't extremely demanding. I had hoped to work at Morehouse for a long time. One day I was leaving the campus in our car on my way to a Bible study. Little did I know that a block party was being hosted in the middle of the campus, and I had to drive through it to leave. As I slowly drove the car into the crowd, one guy banged his hand on the hood and started jawing at me. I showed my work ID, thinking he was a student, but he didn't care. It seemed like a lot of the crowd was made up of people who shouldn't have been on campus. At that moment, another guy reached his hand into the car window as if to grab me, but I couldn't push the car forward because of the crowd. At that point, I made a decision that got me out of the raucous crowd but cost me my job in the process. Looking at the young man next to my window, I put my handgun (legally owned) on the dash of my car. Quickly, he took his hand out of the window, the guy banging on the hood moved away, the crowd cleared out, and I drove on through. As soon as I got through the crowd, I called campus police to report the incident. Looking back on it now, I should have called them to get the crowd dispersed instead of acting like Clint Eastwood over the whole incident. If I could go back and get a do-over on that day, I would handle it much differently.

While I didn't break any laws, it was far from my best moment as a leader at Morehouse. I was asked to resign a few weeks later. I lost my income, and we lost our home. It was a mess all around.

However, I made up my mind then and there that I would use that setback as an opportunity to start new ventures of my own. While I found myself in an unplanned crisis at the time, the best work of my professional life happened after I stepped down at Morehouse. If you happen to lose your job, think about these things:

1. Whatever comes next, you are going to have to work harder than you ever have in your life. Finding a new job is more difficult than it's ever been, and starting your own thing is twice as hard as working for someone else.

2. Use your fresh start as an opportunity to reinvent yourself. Make your résumé and LinkedIn profile reflect who

it is you are aiming to become. This is what I did after I left my job at Morehouse. I decided that social media and activism were going to be my main thing. I also started grad school at Emory University.

3. Always be developing new skills, like Web coding, that make you valuable to an ever-changing marketplace.

4. Don't burn any bridges. If you get let go, leave with grace and dignity, and try to keep all your relationships in working order.

When You Are Depressed

Depression is a real thing. For most of my adult life, I thought I was immune to it. I've always worked my way through hard times and recovered well. One time, though, several years ago, the charity I was working for in Haiti suffered cutbacks and had to let me go, the start-up that I founded and sold to investors fired me and our small staff, and I resigned from the church I started and loved in inner-city Atlanta after a disagreement with our board about the direction I was taking the church, all in the span of a few days. Soon, I found myself so low that I really didn't know how to find my way out. Before I knew to ask for help or to get guidance from friends or mentors, I was already in a brutally low place. Having placed so much of my value and self-worth in what I did for a living, I didn't know how to see myself without the jobs I knew and loved so much. I no longer wanted to leave the house or even my home office for that matter. I'm pretty sure I quit shaving and maybe even bathing for a few days until my wife forced me to clean up. Lonely, confused, and feeling stuck, I reached out to people for help, but a lot of them didn't even respond.

I thank God to this day for my wife, my family, and a few close friends who loved me through that hard time, and I am particularly thankful for Dave Gibbons, a kind soul in California who saw my broken state and was determined to love me through it. Dave helped move my family from Atlanta to Southern California and gave us several months to heal through counseling and some work that I really loved. He also encouraged me to pursue the dreams that were in my heart and gave me the base to consider those dreams. I'm convinced I might still be stuck in a basement somewhere wearing five-year-old underwear if Dave hadn't had such compassion for me during that time.

If you find yourself depressed or really far down in the dumps, here are a few things you can do:

1. Get help. If your insurance covers it, get professional help. Even seeking pastoral counseling is a good thing. You really can't find your way out of it on your own.

2. Tell your friends and family about your troubles. Have at least one loved one whom you fully confide in so that you aren't all alone in the world.

3. Don't make any permanent decisions based on temporary circumstances. I've had friends commit suicide over

situations that would have passed in just a few days, but they couldn't see that in the fog of depression.

4. Don't be ashamed. Many people have been through this and recovered, and you will, too.

When Someone You Love Dies

We don't really bounce back from the loss of a loved one. Regardless of your religious beliefs, few things take the wind out of our lives like someone we love's passing away. It changes us and permanently creates a new world in which that person is completely absent except for our priceless memories of them. It doesn't matter that we all know it's a fate we will someday meet; it just flat-out hurts to lose a loved one. I've counseled many families through grief and have stood there with my own family and friends as we lost our loved ones to violence, cancer, disease, old age, accidents, and more. It's never easy. At first, it may take all you have to simply breathe and sleep and occasionally eat. Eventually you may find yourself able to leave the house and go to the store. One day you may go to a play or a movie. Just keep on living.

When I was a freshman at Morehouse College I was dating Rai, but we were pretty serious. In the middle of the night, she called me crying uncontrollably. In the span of a day, two of her aunts, each a sister of her mother, died suddenly and unexpectedly in completely separate incidents. As you could imagine, her grandparents and the entire family were deeply wounded to their core. It took real strength for each member of the family to wake up every day knowing that Vicki and Robin were gone.

Here are a few things that I have found can ease the pain just a little:

1. Do not be afraid to cry and mourn and go through the appropriate stages of grief. Holding this back will repress your emotions in a very unhealthy way.

2. Always ask yourself how the person you loved would want you to live your life, and live it in a way that would honor them. This helps most people move forward in life better than any advice anyone could ever give.

3. Be there for your other friends and family who were affected by the loss, and find ways to grieve together. Talk and share wonderful stories with one another.

4. Dedicate one of your 100 life goals to them.

When You Are Sick or Injured

Having been through several spinal surgeries, a brutal car accident, and a life of pretty severe pain, I have a great deal of sympathy for any of you who are experiencing this yourself or are loving someone through a real health challenge. Few things can derail your life from top to bottom like a major health crisis. While my hope is that you never have to face such a thing, health problems happen, and if you do have such a crisis, you absolutely can endure it. As hard or as strange as it may sound, a health crisis can give you a new lease on life if you'll let it. While I'm in pain even as I write this book, my memory of harder times has given me a profound sense of appreciation for every single day I am able to live and walk freely on this earth! If you ever feel tempted to let your health crisis make you bitter, focus instead on all the years of good health you've had or even how your new challenges make you have a real heart for other people in pain.

Here are a few more ideas for how to get through this:

1. Make healing and recovering your top priority. Push yourself as hard as the doctors allow, but do it wisely and within the guidelines you've been given. Having a setback during your recovery process is the last thing you want.

2. Use this time to have a renewed focus on your health and fitness goals, and begin making all the changes and improvements you need to set yourself up for success after you recover.

3. If you happen to be homebound because of your injury, make the most of your time. Study your 100 life goals to see if your extended time at home will allow you to focus on any of your goals that would otherwise be difficult with your normal work schedule. This could be the perfect time to start writing, studying for college entrance exams, or learning a new skill online.

When You Are Having Relationship Issues

Relationship drama is like water to the life-goal fireball—it douses your momentum and stops it dead in its tracks. While I'm all for having tough conversations with friends and family and I understand that real life is full of arguments and fallings-out, when you are determined to live your best life it's important that you avoid unnecessary relationship challenges like the plague. When you have a strong emotional base with dedicated family and friends to do life with, you will not only find life to be much more enjoyable, but you will have a foundation that acts like a springboard to all your life goals.

I get that you don't choose your family. My family has all types of ups and downs just like yours. However, we all choose how we respond to the challenges that life throws our way. Every chance you get, in conflict and out, choose love, peace, and harmony. Without fail, I have found that when my wife and I are thriving in our marriage and when I'm at peace in my key relationships, I'm simply able to focus and get more done day in and day out. Here are a few tips to think about:

1. Consider family counseling for long-standing problems you may be facing. Having an unbiased mediator can make all the difference in the world.

2. Never get physical or hurl insults during conflicts in your relationships. It'd be better for you to walk away than say or do something that you'll regret but can't take back.

3. Sometimes we have friends for a particular phase of life, and when we try to take these friendships into a new phase

it feels like putting a square peg into a round hole. Know that some relationships come to an end, and that's okay.

When You Are in over Your Head

I wish I didn't know so much about being in over my head. Until a few years ago, I had the hardest time saying no to anything that anybody requested of me. For a period of about ten years, I actually accepted every speaking request that was ever made—no matter where it was or who was making it, I said yes. I accepted every board position that came my way. I accepted every request to guest-blog or tweet or consult or advise or do a media interview with no reservation—and it caused *tons* of problems in my life. Ultimately I couldn't keep up with all of the requests, and people would be disappointed when I didn't keep my word—which wasn't great for my reputation. With a growing list of demands, a huge family, and sometimes two or three full-time jobs pulling me in a gazillion different directions, I was setting myself up for a real meltdown . . . until I learned that part of being a competent and mature leader meant saying no gracefully when I had to. Ultimately, it's better for others when I say no to something I just can't do, giving them a chance to move on, than it is for me to say yes and disappoint them when I underperform.

I've had many situations where I took on too much work or too many responsibilities and just felt completely overwhelmed with life. It's a terrible feeling, and sometimes it's nearly impossible to escape. Sometimes my wife and I have foster children that we add to our already huge mix of four kids, and it can be very stressful—particularly if we are fostering a baby. During those times it's important that everybody is carrying their workload and stepping up in every way possible. Other times, when life requires you to work more than one job or you have to be in multiple

Being busy isn't the same as being successful.

places at once because of family or school responsibilities, you just have to ride the wave until it's over, knowing that it won't always be that way. Regardless of the position you find yourself in, I have several tips that I think could really make a difference for you:

1. Understand that being busy isn't the same as being successful. Learn to say no to everything that isn't really a perfect use of your time. Your time is a limited commodity and must be used well if you're going to be healthy and achieve your 100 life goals.

2. Use something like Google Calendar to map out your day. This will eliminate surprises and give you a clear understanding of what to expect day by day and week by week. Part of feeling overwhelmed is keeping too much stuff in your head that can be written down or put online so that you can focus on what matters.

3. If you've messed up somehow by taking on too much work and you know that you can't do it on your own, do the hard thing of either asking for help or letting people know that you have to gracefully bow out of the task at hand in order for it to get done.

4. Sometimes you have to audit your own life and make

tough decisions to remove previous commitments and responsibilities. While it may indeed be better to stop commitments you can't keep before you actually make them, life happens. Once in a blue moon it may be required of you to hit control-alt-delete on almost everything so that you can have a fresh start.

When You Are in Legal Trouble

Whether you're at fault or being wrongly accused of something you didn't do, being in any type of legal trouble is a nightmare that can zap your budget and derail your life if you're not careful. Whether it's something domestic, like a bankruptcy or foreclosure, or something much more serious, like a pending lawsuit or a criminal charge, this is one area of your life where putting your head in the sand can have dire consequences. I've walked with several friends through every type of legal case you could imagine and have a few bits of advice on how you can handle legal challenges well.

1. Seek the best legal advice you can afford. If you cannot afford an attorney, ask your closest friends and family members if they know an attorney who can guide you through the key decisions you need to make. Also search online to see if your city has a legal aid society made up of volunteer attorneys.

2. Be proactive. Avoiding legal issues almost always makes the consequences worse and will undoubtedly make dealing with them more expensive.

3. If by chance you have broken the law and have pending charges, this may sound obvious, but stop doing what has gotten you in trouble if you haven't done so already. Anything that you could be doing that has the potential to make your case any worse needs to end immediately.

When You Are About to Give Up

I've described lots of challenges that you could face, but you and I know that the list could go on and on and on. Maybe I've described something that is jamming you up right here and now, or maybe you are facing adversities that are uniquely your own. Whatever the case may be, don't give up!

Never stop pursuing your 100 life goals.

Never stop living your best life.

Never stop growing.

Never stop pushing your limits to the max.

Maybe you feel like you have the weight of the world on your shoulders right now, or maybe you are so tired of failure that giving up just seems worth it. I understand. I assure you I do. I have had my back against the wall more times than I can count. When your tank is empty and you've done everything that you know how to do, I have three things I'd like for you to earnestly consider. They've worked for me time after time after time.

1. Pray. Maybe you aren't religious, or you're unsure how you feel about God. I understand. All I know is that across the years when I felt like I had nowhere else to turn and I

chose to pray to God, I felt a real sense of relief. When my entire face was ripped to shreds in the car accident and I couldn't open my eyes for days because they were swollen shut, all I really knew to do was pray, and it made all the difference. It wasn't that God took all the pain away, but I never felt like I was alone.

2. Google "famous survival stories," and be amazed. Click around and read stories from more than one link. Sometimes it helps to know that other human beings have faced incredibly long odds, even longer than you may be facing, and lived to tell the tale. The human will to live is an amazing thing, and I think you'll find at least one story that motivates you.

3. This may sound a little weird, but it helps me to remember that I come from hundreds of generations of people who had to fight tooth and nail to survive on this planet. It doesn't matter which continent your immediate ancestry comes from—each and every one of us goes back thousands and thousands and thousands of years to some type of original people. I'm not trying to minimize what you may be up against right now, but allow your mind to take a quick stroll through history to imagine what all our lineage had to endure just for you and me to show up today. We were born to survive and thrive on this planet!

DEEP REWARDS

I'm not here to tell you that adversity is loads of fun and that you should love it as much as you would your favorite dessert, but few things are as deeply rewarding as overcoming it. As I reflect back on my personal and professional life, some successes stand out, but no memories are as crystallized and cherished as the many recoveries from setbacks. Navigating your way through the low moments will build character and resiliency like nothing else can, and if your team can stay together during the greatest times of challenge, you'll be exponentially stronger and more connected for it on the other side.

CONCLUSION

ongratulations! I am so stinking proud of you. This is not an easy book to complete. If you've made it this far, you have taken real steps toward changing the way you live your life from this point forward. Over the next few weeks and months, and certainly over the next few years, things will continue to develop and shift in your life. Circumstances will come and go—some more difficult than others—and you will hopefully learn to adapt and become stronger. As a result, you will probably have a few life goals that you are going to change your mind about. Your views will grow organically over time, and this means that many of your goals will change and grow as well. This is fine. Always feel free to adjust and update your goals as you see fit, as long as you don't lose sight of your dreams and give up! I only ask that if you tinker with a goal or replace it altogether, pledge to make the new goal bigger and bolder than what you're replacing. Never replace a goal simply because it seems too hard or because the rough times of life have made dreaming about your future more and more difficult. Keep the larger picture in mind.

Hear my heart—I'm all for having unplanned moments in life, but when you make a decision to live life on purpose with a clear sense of mission and direction, it's a game changer. No more will entire months and years, decades even, pass by without your accomplishing what you were put on the earth to do. You have so much potential to not only change your own life, but to make an enormous impact on the entire world. Inside of you is strength and power and ingenuity that you haven't even tapped into yet, and I can't wait to see what happens when you do.

I am hopeful that we can stay in touch, and I want to offer my support for you along your journey. Here are a few key ways we can stay connected. If for some reason one option isn't working, try another, but I'll make sure I always stay accessible to encourage you every chance I get.

To contact Shaun King, please try any of the below:
Cell Phone Number: (404) 461-9850
E-mail: shaun@100lifegoals.com
Twitter: @ShaunKing

ACKNOWLEDGMENTS

When I first finished this manuscript, my wife clowned on me, because I wrote the longest thank-you note of all time acknowledging dozens of people who have helped make this book possible. I certainly did not get this far on my own, and I am incredibly grateful to each and every person who has helped encourage and guide me along the way. If you are reading this sentence and know that you've been in my corner, thank you so much. I do, though, have to mention a few essential people who have specifically helped me complete this book.

I'd like to thank my literary agent, Shannon Litton, for being an early and persistent believer in my ability to write and publish this book. Shannon, this book and the change it will bring would not be possible without you.

I'd like to thank my primary editor, Jessica Wong, for taking 70,000 rough words and smoothing them over into something I can be proud of. You made my ideas flow so much better and did it in record time.

Thanks to the entire team at Howard Books for taking a shot on a guy like me. Your support and belief in me means the world.

Thanks to my wife, Rai, and the kids (Tae, Kendi, EZ, and Savannah) for being so amazingly patient and supportive during the months it took me to complete this project. I couldn't ask for a more loving and supportive family. I love you all so very much.

ABOUT THE AUTHOR

Now a full-time author and teacher through Life Goals University, Shaun King is one of the most respected social entrepreneurs and humanitarians in the world. An award-winning leader, Shaun is widely regarded as one of today's most dynamic voices on how social media and a little bit of courage can make our world a radically better place. He speaks a message of hope and action over 150 times a year, has appeared in over 100 national and international press outlets, started and sold three tech companies, raised over $5 million for causes all over the world, and won the coveted Mashable Award for Most Creative Social Good Campaign.

Shaun is married to his high school sweetheart, Rai. Their young family, which changes in size often because of adoptions and foster children, currently lives in Los Angeles, but over the past few years they have called Cape Town, South Africa; Atlanta; Kentucky; and Manhattan home. The entire King family loves to travel and has currently visited thirty-five of the United States in their family goal of visiting all fifty together.

Get email updates on

SHAUN KING,

exclusive offers,

and other great book recommendations

from Simon & Schuster.

Visit **newsletters.simonandschuster.com**

or

scan below to sign up:

CPSIA information can be obtained
at www.ICGtesting.com
Printed in the USA
LVOW12s0025240118
563793LV00001B/86/P

9 781476 790183